T0104503

MOTHER ALWAYS SAID, "..."

ROBERT POPOVICH

authorHOUSE®

AuthorHouse™
1663 Liberty Drive
Bloomington, IN 47403
www.authorhouse.com
Phone: 833-262-8899

Mother Always Said, ". . ." is a work of non-fiction—several names have been change to protect individual privacy.

Published by AuthorHouse 04/27/2022

ISBN: 978-1-4918-9807-9 (sc)
ISBN: 978-1-4918-9806-2 (hc)
ISBN: 978-1-4918-9805-5 (e)

Library of Congress Control Number: 2014905396

Print information available on the last page.

This book is printed on acid-free paper.

IN LOVING MEMORY OF . . .

MY MOTHER, DOROTHY,
AND HER MENTOR AND SURROGATE FATHER
—MORRIS CHAMOVITZ

ACKNOWLEDGMENTS

Family

TO MY MOTHER DOROTHY, who without her guidance, love and strength, this book would not have been possible. To my *father Theodore* who taught me the value of hard work and education are the keys to open life's unlimited opportunities. To my *brother Charles*, whose unwavering support has been a constant source of inspiration throughout my life.

TO MY MOTHER'S MENTOR AND SURROGATE FATHER, MORRIS CHAMOVITZ whose business acumen is only exceeded by his faith, humanity, generosity and wisdom. I was fortunate to be in his presence and learn invaluable lessons that were the foundation of my mother's success and a guiding light for my future. He was a man of honor, trust and respect, and who unselfishly, and anonymously, gave to those less fortunate. I asked him once, "Mr. Chamovitz, what is a wealthy man?" He smiled, and said without hesitation, *"A truly wealthy man is someone who has his faith, health, family, no debt and five dollars in his pocket."* He then added, "The only indebtedness a man should have is his gratitude to God for all of his blessings . . . and that is a debt that can never be repaid, or one you should never want to repay." His word was his bond, and his bond was his faith.

TO MY WIFE LYNN, I offer my heartfelt gratitude for her patience, love and understanding, and for being an incomparable mother, loving grandmother, and whose heart can be measured by her years of dedication to her church, friends, community and those less fortunate. Her unselfishness and kindness to others is a model for anyone to admire and follow. To her parents, *Dewey* and *Jean Vanich,* I express my appreciation for their caring and kindness as in-laws and as loving grandparents. To *Doris* and *Bob*

Dudley, lifetime neighbors and friends, and adopted grandparents to our children, and whose love and support are the true measure of their hearts.

TO MY SONS DEJAN ALEXANDER POPOVICH, AND STEVAN DAMIAN POPOVICH, who would make any parent burst with pride for each of their individual accomplishments; and more importantly, for their moral and ethical foundation that guides them in every aspect of their lives. Their dedication to their family and friends are the true measure of their character and souls.

TO OUR DAUGHTER-IN-LAW, JORDANA ROSEN POPOVICH, who we consider the daughter we never had. Our love and respect for her unwavering devotion as a wife, mother and daughter-in-law, including her stellar academic achievements, and chosen profession, dedicated to the health and welfare of others, are all and more anyone could hope or deserve to enjoy.

TO OUR GRANDDAUGHTER, SYDNEY MICHELLE ROSEN POPOVICH, who turned five years of age on January 10, 2014, and is the light that brightens every aspect of all of our lives each and every day. Life is filled with many gifts, but none like that of a grandchild whose innocence and unconditional love teaches us what is truly important in life—the love of family and the gift of life.

TO MY NEPHEWS, KEVIN, CHRISTOPHER AND RICHARD who have always been a source of pride, along with their children, *Haley, Charlie, Nicholas, Alexis* and *Abigail;* to my maternal grandmother *Lillian*, and paternal grandmother *Juka* for their unconditional love and timeless wisdom; to my aunts *Mary, Ann, Martha, Mildred, Daisy and Joanne* and uncles, *Theodore* and *Rudy* for their humility and generosity; to my cousins, and their spouses, *Tony and Gene; Donny, Johnny* and *Tommy; Richard, Ronnie, Michael* and *Dawn Marie; Kathy* and *Dean; David Allen and Daryl Robert* none of whom fell far from the tree of love and caring for family and all others in their lives.

A SPECIAL ACKNOWLEDGMENT TO MY COUSIN PATRICIA, who was the sister I never had, and whose accomplishments are only exceeded by her generosity, and to my Cousin *Lillian* who mirrored her mother's energy and will to succeed, no matter the circumstances, and that love of family comes before all else. This is a family filled with love and thoughtfulness, all of whom I couldn't be more proud and grateful to be a part of their lives.

TO MY UNCLE MONTGOMERY, a surrogate father, his loving wife *Kay* and my cousins *Teddy* and *Melanie,* all of whom set a standard for faith, family and education that were guideposts throughout my formative years.

Education and Faith

TO MRS. CHARLOTTE BACON, my second grade teacher, at Jones School in Aliquippa, PA, who taught me that, we are not measured by our race, gender or religion, but by our contributions to faith, family and community. To *Richard Drake and Dennis Miller*, childhood friends that offered a lifetime of wonderful memories and unwavering support. To the *Very Reverend Father Vlastimir Tomich*, who taught me that we are all God's children of equal value and importance. To *Mrs. Andreyev*, my high school English teacher who opened my eyes to the beauty of literature, poetry and the power of words. To the *Very Reverend Stevan Stepanov*, his wife *Ana*, and their children *Ivana* and *Marko* for their lifetime service to our parish, and without whom we never would have accomplished so much. To *Mrs. Natalie Rebich*, a teacher, inspirational leader, choir director, and whose love of music, and passion for life and faith enriched all of our lives, and to her husband *Eli* whose contributions to family and faith make all of us proud. *To the St. Elijah Parish, Serbian Orthodox Church parishioners,* my gratitude for their love and support throughout the years for me and my family. Life without faith is like a ship without a rudder. To the *Gunjak* and *Tomic* families who came to this country with their unwavering faith, second to none work ethic, intelligence and determination succeeded against all odds.

Editor

TO MY EDITOR, JILL CUENI-COHEN, I want to offer my eternal gratitude for her knowledge, talents and determination she so unselfishly applied to every aspect of this project. I am fortunate to know her as a friend, colleague, and fellow lover of poetry and words. Her ability to effortlessly enhance a writer's voice, but without losing its identity is a marvel in and of itself. She is the light at the end of the tunnel for any author or writer who demands excellence by any standard of measure.

Friends and Colleagues

TO JOHN BUNCE, whom I admire for his intellectual capacity to bring lucidity and objectivity to any issue of value in life. He is a colleague, confidant and spiritual adviser of the first order. His ability to seamlessly weave faith with functionality in a complex world is a quality few possess. His voice of reason and sensitivity, are only exceeded by his humility driven by his faith and desire to improve the lives of others. I give thanks everyday for him being part of my life, and I am certain, I speak for countless others as well. To his wife *Nancy*, and daughters, *Emily, M.D.* and *Abigail* who are the reflection of a family filled with faith and achievement, and my heartfelt thanks to *Michael Freker,* a colleague and friend, whose support in all aspects of my endeavors is so greatly appreciated.

TO PAM GREGG, a lifetime friend, and whose touch for creativity and uncompromising high standards in theater direction, and in life, are admired by all who know her.

TO THE SEWICKLEY COMMUNITY AT LARGE, it is often said, it takes a community to raise a child to develop into becoming a mature, responsible, caring and accomplished individual, and equally important, to give back to those who have supported them all of their lives. The Sewickley community and Sewickley Academy have done just that, they played a critical role in contributing to our son's character as responsible individuals and citizens of the world.

TO BARBARA YOUNG MORRIS, who is an admired intellect and humanitarian, in all aspects of her life. She is a friend, colleague, and advisor, and an irreplaceable 'sounding board,' who offers a fresh and valued perspective in helping me effectively and efficiently deal with the complexities in my career.

TO TOM MCKENZIE, a lifetime friend, art teacher extraordinaire, and guiding light for his students, and his well-documented contributions to the service men and women, who so unselfishly protect our freedoms at great personal sacrifice—we are forever in your debt.

I also want to acknowledge the countless individuals who have contributed significantly to my knowledge and career throughout the who must remain nameless given the sensitivity of their work, and continue to give of themselves with their efforts only known to a few. Sacrifice comes in many different forms, and too many consider, anonymity the greatest test of humility and commitment to a cause.

Mentors

TO MS. DOROTHEA FRANCIS, my first working supervisor whose guidance was invaluable in shaping my perspective of business and its social responsibility.

TO GEORGE EYESMONT III, a fellow Russian military intelligence analyst, who I served with during the height of the US/Soviet Cold War, for his guidance, support, mentoring, and most of all, in shaping my character and realizing the only limitations in life are self-imposed.

TO INGRID AND FRITZ OSWALD, who took me under wing when I first moved to West Germany and embraced me as a son and played a vital role in supporting my work objectives in my career.

TO TOM KIRKWOOD, a colleague, friend and intellectual, whose humility and talents are only exceeded by his generosity to all that are a part of his life. We shared a journey through West Berlin and West

Germany filled with adventures, challenges and shared moments of joy, and in some instances, roads less traveled. My admirations for his talent and humanity have been a constant source of inspiration.

TO MY COLLEAGUES AND FRIENDS WITHIN THE US, GERMAN AND RUSSIAN GOVERNMENTS, who taught me that the first and most important lesson in international diplomacy, is working in the best interest of all parties. To all of my countless clients over the years, who gave me the opportunity to live my dream as an international business and political consultant, I am forever in your debt.

As Mother Always Said, " . . ." *faith* is the measure of our *hearts*; *intellect* is the measure of our *abilities*; *giving* is the measure of our *generosity*; and *life* is a *blessing* to us all."

LIFE OFFERS PASSION

Poet: Robert Popovich © 1/6/04

We are born one day with fanfare and kind,
But we too quickly learn—there is so little time.

We are taught life's lessons from those near and far,
Hoping they serve us well—in search of our star.

We experience the best and worst with nary a warning,
In hopes of more laughter—than despair and mourning.

So with all of this uncertainty what does life truly offer,
It is the choice of 'passion'—over predictability and order.

For in living with passion, we can be certain of one thing,
We will have tasted life's grapes—whether sweet or vinegary.

And when our lives have ended, and it is all said and done,
Our degree of passion—will determine our life's total sum.

TO THE MOTHERS OF THE WORLD

MUCH HAS BEEN WRITTEN of your contributions, but most efforts to describe them have failed to capture their essence. From cleanliness to faith, from guidance to education, from adversity to resolution, from hope to reality, and from discipline to love, you have filled every void and softened every fall. With this in mind, we hold on to what has been so dear to us, but at the same time struggle to establish our independence and demonstrate that, your efforts were not in vain.

Your selfless ability to do so much for so many, while denying yourself, is too often rewarded by taking you for granted. Although we celebrate your deeds on a national day of honor, we frequently forget that it is the small acknowledgments of appreciation that you most cherish and desire. Your trust, faith, encouragement and love serve as a constant reminder of what is truly important in life.

To all the mothers of the world from all the children of the world for all you have done and all that is yet to come, we simply want to say, "Thank you."

READER TESTIMONIALS . . .

"You were very thoughtful to send me a copy of your new book, in which you so effectively, and warmly, deal with family values and their role in our Nation's future." **First Lady Barbara Bush**

"The beauty of Mother always said, " . . ." is in its simplicity. It takes complex human emotional issues and deals with them in an entertaining but practical manner. A must read for people of all ages. **Kent L. Brown, Publisher, Highlights for Children Boyds Mill Press**

"It was a delight to read your book . . . I am a grandmother myself and could see myself in many of the situations." **Sophie Masloff, (former) Mayor, City of Pittsburgh**

"Mother always said, " . . ." reflects family values that are critical to the future of our country." **C.F.Fetterolf, former, President & CEO—ALCOA Corporation**

"A most delightful book . . . full of wit and witticism and so many wonderful lessons to be learned for us all." **Mim Bizic, Gifted Teacher, Sewickley, PA**

"I was your second grade teacher and want to congratulate you on your book . . . it is an excellent tribute to your mother and all mothers who encourage and inspire their children to make the right choices and develop their talents to the fullest. **Mrs. Charlotte M.Bacon, Sewickley, PA**

"How you honor our family by writing so respectfully and lovingly of my father. You have a flare for expressing yourself in an intimate and warm fashion . . . without getting saccharin or gushy . . . as we say in Hebrew,

"I am a captive of indebtedness." **David L. Chamovitz, M.D. (son of Morris) Tel Aviv, Israel**

"I started reading it and couldn't put it down—done at 2am. Your style of writing is unlike I have read before . . . its shall by my guide in my career." **Lisa Ellerin, Teacher**

'We keep losing the 'truths' that previous generations have taught us, and you've reminded us all in a way that is not pedantic or imposing. It is light, refreshing and certainly manageable in every sense of the word." **Father Tom Newsholtz, St. Timothy's Episcopal Church, Falls Church, VA**

"This is the kind of basic wisdom that should be practiced by politicians-truly enjoyed it." **Jim Moody, former, Member of Congress—Wisconsin**

"As a bookseller, I enjoy being able to recommend books like yours. It is witty and very readable, but also carries an important message of importance. It never preaches; it guides the reader to the point the same way mothers guide children awareness gently, but firmly. **Kathleen Stratton Smith, Borders Book Shop**

"This book crosses on international borders—it reflects the best of all cultures and that in itself is worth the read." **Alexej Novachev, President, Bank Veda St. Petersburg, Russia**

"The wisdom of Dorothy Popovich summons to our souls a love full of decency, practicality and common sense in a world that she recognized to be often hostile and cynical. Robert's stories of his mother wonderfully capture the heart of her indomitable goodness. **John Bunce, former US Naval Officer and Entrepreneur**

I indeed enjoyed Mother Always Said, ". . ." The book took much longer to read partly because I found myself not wanting to go to the next chapter to allow the current chapter's message and theme to soak in . . . to allow time to absorb how the message relates to my life (an examination of consciousness if you will) . . . to meditate . . . to take that particular chapter into the day and let the day and the message interact . . . a kind of synergy. This response is unlike any other I have had to a book, other than a spiritually branded book. This is a book, which is unusually value-added. I do see this book in business although I would never have guessed so before starting the book. The learning moment opportunities are at least as numerous as the chapters. **Richard McCormack, CEO, Humaneering Corp.**

CONTENTS

INTRODUCTION

IN 1980, I WORKED AS a free-lance marketing consultant in New York City. Fresh out of the relatively secure and predictable corporate world, I eagerly looked forward to an entrepreneurial future that held seemingly limitless potential, but also great uncertainty and intense competition. Even though I had a relatively successful corporate career, which translates into *Never having been fired*, I was experiencing a classic case of mixed feelings. As a result, it is not difficult to understand my sense of urgency in wanting to move forward as quickly as possible to avoid any second thoughts about a decision that at the time was irreversible. During my second week of independence, I was having lunch with an old client and friend who presented me with my first window of opportunity.

He had many contacts in private industry, as well as high-level governmental contacts in Europe. He asked if I would be interested in speaking at a business conference in West Germany. Without hesitation, I accepted. He went on to say that the original speaker canceled, and the conference coordinator was desperate.

I tried to ignore the implication that they would take anyone at this point, and turned my attention to asking obvious questions. Who was the *audience* and what were their expectations? What *topic* should I cover and for how long? Each question was met with either a shrug of the shoulders, or the same response—he had no idea. The only information he had in his possession was the name of the conference leader, the city, the date, and where I would be staying. All other details would be provided upon my arrival. He tried to reassure me that all would go well. He almost forgot to mention one minor detail—my flight was later that evening.

Under normal circumstances, I might have been more concerned about the topic and audience, but with little time to spare, those details would have to wait. I rushed to my apartment and packed only the essentials—my passport, a change of clothes, toothbrush and a Berlitz German phrase book.

As I traveled to the airport and boarded my flight to Frankfurt, my mind was racing. All I could think about was the incredible opportunity I had been handed. However, I had forgotten one of Mother's more profound and critical pearls of wisdom: *Nothing is ever as good as it seems, or as bad as it seems.*

Jetlagged but excited, I walked through one of those endless international arrival corridors, cleared customs and was on my way out of the airport, when I spotted a sign bearing my name in the hands of a man dressed in a chauffeur's uniform.

He looked about as nervous as I felt as he led me towards the waiting Mercedes Benz limousine courtesy car. It was plush inside and well appointed with all the luxuries—a telephone, a bar, a writing desk and all sorts of other hidden amenities; putting my new powder-blue Super Beetle Volkswagen to shame.

"How long will it take to reach the conference center?" I asked the driver as we pulled onto the Autobahn.

"One hour," he stated, smugly adding in his thick German accent, "I believe that would be perhaps two hours in the United States? Ja?" Moments later, we were cruising in excess of 100 miles per hour, and I suddenly understood what he meant. The countryside was a beautiful blur.

As we pulled into the conference center driveway, I noticed a stately looking man anxiously pacing the area near the driveway. Intense relief filled his face when he saw me seated in the back seat. Even before we came to a complete stop, he grabbed the door handle, pulled the door open, reached in as if to shake my hand, and pulled me out of the car. "Thank goodness you're here!" he said, grinning a bit manically. "You go on in ten minutes." "Who is the audience and what are their expectations?" I asked, gulping the air a bit too quickly as the fear caught in my throat.

"High-level executives to first-line supervisors from ten European nations," was his answer. Further questioning uncovered the awful truth: the audience was *sorely* disappointed that the original speaker—a former Noble Prize—fell ill, and an unknown, last-minute substitute would be taking his place. At that point, my pulse was pumping at somewhere near the speed of light, which I assumed to be a precursor to hyperventilation. I knew I was up the proverbial creek without a paddle.

I searched my mind for a psychological life preserver, and the sound of my mother's voice filled my head. She said, *"Robert, run to the problem, not away from it. It can be a great opportunity if you know how to take advantage of it."* A feeling of calm and certainty replaced my high-anxiety and self-doubt.

Standing on a stage in front of at least 200 ticked-off attendees, I took a deep breath and began with, "Mother always said, 'Robert, asking good questions is like eating a lot of fish—they both develop great minds.'"

The audience began murmuring, and their attention towards me soon turned from distrust to curiosity and apparent agreement. I had found a common denominator—everyone has a mother; and most people would probably agree that they have learned valuable lessons from their mothers.

Relief washed over me, and so I offered another tidbit of wisdom, which was well received, so I kept the quotes coming, adding in adolescent and career anecdotes to illustrate their value. My message was this: In business, as in life, great wisdom can come from the most humble of sources.

My mother, Dorothy Popovich, was a woman with little formal schooling. However, she taught me more about how to succeed in business and as an individual, than all my years of schooling and the writings of a multitude of recognized authorities.

The more I shared of my mother with the audience, the more they showed their appreciation by laughing and nodding throughout my presentation. The original hour I was slotted to speak suddenly turned into two; yet no one seemed to notice or care. What I did notice was the fact that my mother's teachings had transformed a culturally diverse audience into a homogeneous one.

At the conclusion of my presentation, many of them made it a point to stop and share stories about their own mothers. It was Mothers Day out of season, and a day that shaped the rest of my consulting career.

Over the past two decades, I have found colleagues, clients and friends the world over equally delighted by my mother's maxims and how they applied them in their lives. Many of them encouraged me to write a book about her teachings so that others might benefit.

In citing my own experiences as my sources, I am not claiming that my mother or I coined all of these phrases. Some are original, while others are adaptations of well-known maxims from great philosophers and individuals representing many different cultures and societies. My goal is to illustrate how these messages have affected my life and provide a source of inspiration for others to reflect upon and potentially apply in their own lives.

I dedicate this book to *all* the mothers of the world for their unselfish and tireless efforts to nurture, guide and protect their children. All they want in return for their devotion is love and respect.

Professional women of the world who have forged new ground by taking their rightful place in every segment of business and society, I applaud them as well. My mother was a charter member of your club when a woman's individual rights and potential did not receive their deserved status. To every mother's child, I offer this personal diary of growing up with my mother, in hopes you might one day revisit yours.

PROLOGUE

My MOTHER WAS THE THIRD-OLDEST CHILD in a family of nine brothers and sisters. Born in 1918, she was a product of her proud Serbian-American heritage and values that gave her a strong work ethic and devotion to family. This commitment was tested at an early age when her father unexpectedly died. She had little choice but to drop out of school, in order to contribute to supporting the family. She willingly accepted her fate, and in time came to realize her real-life education and experiences would far surpass many formal equivalents.

Growing up, I often wondered how my mother came to work in a shoe store. Then I decided to ask the owner, Mr. Morris Chamovitz, my mother's mentor and surrogate father, that very question.

"One day," he said with pride, "a young, innocent, beautiful and determined-looking girl entered my store seeking employment, and she explained there was a situation in her family, which dictated that she find a job.

Mr. Chamovitz told me how he pointed out to her that many others were facing similar difficulties, so she changed her tactics.

"I'm honest, hardworking, attend church every week, and I always show respect to others," She told him, but he still was not convinced. He wanted something more, so she made him an offer: "What if I work for you free for one month, and then you can tell me what I'm worth?" Impressed, he hired her on the spot.

After only a week, Morris' partner Harry Jackson called her a 'diamond in the rough.' "I vote for waiving the trial period and recommended hiring her immediately," he told Morris.

Morris, however, did not agree, because as he often said, "A deal is a deal. If you give your word, you are expected to keep it. He saw this as her first and most important lesson in business: *live up to your word*. It was the beginning of a lifelong personal and business relationship that changed both of their lives forever.

Thus Mother learned an invaluable lesson, which took the form of her many maxims—"Robert, run to adversity, not away from it. It's your greatest opportunity if you know how to take advantage of it." When you run away, you lose something far more important than just the immediate "contest." You also lose self-respect, and this is the heaviest loss of all. However, when you confront adversity head-on, you gain something much more valuable than any tangible prize such as a job or money. You gain self-esteem and pride. You become a stronger and more effective person; in addition, sometimes you gain tangible rewards as well. *(Incidentally, my mother received full back pay after she was permanently hired!)*

IMAGE

Mother always said, "Robert . . .
don't forget what your last name is;
you represent all of us,
not just yourself."

EVERY MORNING WHEN I LEFT for school or went out to play, Mother would holler before I was out of earshot, "Don't forget what your last name is; you represent all of us, not just yourself!" Certainly, such messages were to some extent were intended to warn me to "behave." In a staunchly religious Eastern Orthodox family, respect and good behavior topped the list of life's rules, and breaking those rules were considered a relative capital offense, which meant severe verbal admonitions that bordered on inquisitions. No matter how harsh the words, however, they were delivered in a lesson format that required behavioral modifications if privileges were to be restored.

Our Western Pennsylvania community, a suburb of Pittsburgh was a true melting pot of Europeans who came to America. Serbians, Greeks, Italians, Jews, Poles and other Eastern European groups settled in this steel town. Cleanliness, honesty, respect and hard work were the value cornerstones of all these groups.

As I approached the transitional period from boyhood to manhood, I was ready one day for the usual refrain. As I went out the door on my way to school, Mother shouted, "Robert, have a nice day and don't forget . . ." Before she could finish, I said, "Excuse me, Mother. I know it by heart. 'Don't forget what my last name is,' Right?" Her immediate reaction was one of surprise, followed by a rather smug but approving smile. Her reaction led me to ask, "Did I say something funny?" She replied, "No. Just think it only took you thirteen years to remember!"

She went on to say that each of us individually accountable for our actions, and remember that each person's behavior reflects on the family and community. In small ethnic communities, news travels fast, especially bad news, especially when it came to tarnishing the family name.

The shoe store where my mother worked had developed an excellent reputation over the years. Although the store did not have a written mission statement, known for providing high-quality shoes at a reasonable price. In this, it was not unlike other stores, except it stood far above its competitors when it came to customer serve and overall flexibility. That commitment translated into personalized attention, no matter how big or small the purchase. Any complaint was met with immediate action and customer-accepted resolution.

One day after running several errands for my mother, I returned to my mother's store, when in walked a customer that demanding to see a salesperson. My mother walked over to him and asked if she could be of help. It was during the holiday season, which meant the store was brimming with happy holiday shoppers. He responded in a loud and irritable voice, "Yes! I bought these shoes here and they fell apart. I DEMAND A FULL REFUND!" His voice was so loud, everyone in the store turned to identifying its source.

Ignoring his outburst, Mother carefully examined the shoes—*their condition was pre-Civil War.* She then asked if he had a receipt—*an etched stone tablet would have been more like it.* This did not lessen his demand. She went on to ask when he bought the shoes—*he couldn't remember.* It became obvious, he was trying to 'bully' his way to getting a refund. In the meantime, a hush fell over the store as everyone waited to see how my mother handled the situation.

She asked him to wait a moment, while she checked with the owner. She explained the situation to Mr. Chamovitz. "Before I give you my opinion, what do you think is the best way to handle it?" She did not hesitate. "Well, I recommend we give him a refund, even though he doesn't have a receipt." When Morris asked why, she explained that the store was full of good customers, and the incident drew so much attention, she felt she could turn a negative situation into a positive one. He agreed.

She returned to the customer and thanked him for waiting. "Sir, it is store policy that customers provide a receipt or some type of information to verify that the shoes were purchased here. I'm sure you can understand why we have such a policy, but . . ." Before she continued, he interrupted. "I'VE HEARD ENOUGH . . . I WANT TO SPEAK WITH THE OWNER!" She did not react to his outburst, instead she commonly, but firmly stated, "That won't be necessary, I've spoken with the owner and he's given me permission to give you a full refund, but under one condition." The customer quieted and asked, "What condition?" She said that he would have to fill out his name, address and telephone number for their records. In addition, any future refunds he might request would have to meet the store's policy of having a receipt.

He filled out the information, took the money and immediately left the store without a 'thank you' or any form of acknowledgment. After he left, my teenage mind needed to resolve why she gave him a refund, when it was obvious he was lying. She offered her usual quietly confident smile and explained. "Even though there is a store policy, there were other factors involved. With the number of customers in the store, the situation became an opportunity, not a problem." I asked, "But what's going to happen now that everyone in the store saw you break the store policy? Won't they try and do the same thing on day?"

She reassured me that it was highly unlikely, because most were long-standing customers and knew I was making an exception to rid the store of a less than honest customer. "You see Robert, by stating the store policy, it's very unlikely he'll ever come back; but even if he does, he better have a receipt—not only that, people like him are always trying to take advantage of someone, and rarely try to pull the same trick twice." I was beginning to get the bigger picture. This lesson served me well later in the business world, when being 'right' turned into being 'dead right.'

Everything that each employee says or does paints a portrait, or image, of the company they represent, whether at work or in public. Companies spend millions of dollars to develop a specific image, or brand, of how the market perceives its name, products or services. When we mention a specific name, for example, Coca Cola, an immediate image or experience comes to mind, i.e., the product and its relative quality and value.

Once when speaking before a sales force of a highly regarded lumber company, one of the participants, the company's number one salesperson, raised his hand and shared an unlikely admission, "Robert, I want to ask your opinion about one of my major accounts. Two years ago, he quit doing business with us, and if that wasn't bad enough, ever since then, he's been on a one man's crusade to share with anyone who will listen, the supposed injustice he had to bear." You could hear a pin drop. I was shocked, along with everyone else in the room, including the company's president.

The customer wanted a credit of $2,000 for lumber he claimed he returned. The sales representative said there were no records to support his claim. The conflict turned into a battle of wills, with neither side giving in. As a result, the company lost a major customer, and even worse, he launched a one-man 'mudslinging' campaign against my client.

I decided to share "The Returned Shoes Caper." I stressed it is important for every representative of the company to remember what his or her last name is, i.e., they represent the entire company and not just themselves. I said that even though the sales representative was acting in what he thought was in the company's best interest; unfortunately, it wasn't. The negative impact far outweighed adhering to company policy. I suggested they send a letter from the company president, along with a full refund. It may not guarantee his business would return, but he might give serious thought to ending his negative campaign—and from that point of view, it could be considered investment spending.

At that point, we took a five-minute break. The president took me aside to discuss the situation. He wondered what effect my suggestion would have on his top performer. I said the rep might feel a temporary loss of image among his peers, and a sense that upper management was not pleased with his handling of the account, however, at the same time, there were lessons learned and opportunities were on the horizon. The president agreed. The meeting reconvened, and he took the floor.

"Hindsight is always 20/20," he said, "but let's not dwell on the past, let's focus on the future, which is the present." He went on to say, from this point forward, he wants everyone to complete a thorough cost and benefit analysis to avoid such occurrences in the future. He then thanked the sales rep for his willingness to share his story and the value it brought to the meeting. The audience's applause spoke for itself, while the sales rep breathed a sigh of relief.

He added, "We're going to take Robert's advice, I'm going to send a letter of apology, along with a full refund check with interest. Even though much time has passed, and even if it's highly unlikely we can't regain his business, we can at least hope he stops his mudslinging campaign." He went on to point out the company's success attributed to hard work, honesty and fairness to its customers. His decision was a reflection of their philosophy. The veteran sales representative nodded in agreement. As the president started to sit down, he smiled warmly and said, *"And let's not forget what our last name is . . ."*

REVENGE

Mother always said, "Robert . . .
before setting out on revenge,
first dig two graves—
one for your enemy and one for yourself."

WHEN I WAS APPROXIMATELY TWELVE years of age, our family lived in a wonderful neighborhood. Our home was set on a lush, expansive yard, dotted with fruit trees, including the most delicious red and yellow apple varieties. Each year, we eagerly awaited the coming of fall and the annual apple harvest, but this year would be different . . . .

It all began when our neighbor lodged a complaint against us. Several of our larger trees had branches hanging into her yard, which resulted in many apples falling on her property. We made a sincere attempt to pick them up each day, but it was not enough to keep her lawn apple-free. The situation escalated from polite expressions of dissatisfaction to direct and even hostile confrontations. Then, without explanation, she stopped complaining. My parents were relieved but confused by her sudden turnaround.

During the height of the picking season, we could count on four bushels of apples a day, but over the next two weeks, we reaped half that sum. Then we began noticing a significant absence of apples on the branches that reached into her yard and none on the ground on her side of the property line. I asked Mother, "How could she take them without asking?"

"She probably felt justified," answered Mother. "You see, Robert, none of us likes to feel as though we're doing anything wrong, so we rationalize . . . That is, we make excuses or find reasons for our behavior. It is possibly her way of getting back at us; although she never complained in past years, so maybe she is having difficulties in her life we don't know about. Whatever the reasons, she's made a decision to take them without asking." Her explanation only compounded my frustration.

My brother and I were angry and felt the need to take revenge. We were young, impetuous, and as a result, everything in our lives was a case of black and white. What was right was right, and what was wrong always seemed so obvious.

One day, my parents were discussing the situation, and I felt compelled to voice my opinion. Self-righteously I blurted out, "That woman is a thief and should be punished!" I was shocked when my parents showed little support for—or even a reaction to my outburst. As far as I was concerned, it was an open-and-shut case. The only question in my mind was what kind of punishment or legal actions to take. I voted for calling the police and sharing the news with all of the neighbors and local media.

My mother sensed my extreme dismay and asked, "Robert, are you seeking justice or revenge? What good does it do to call the police? Even if we do, what do you think the consequences might be?" I hated when she did that—always asking logical questions that made me think. Why could it not be as simple as it is on television or in the movies: the good guys are totally right and the bad guys are always wrong—the good guys always won, and justice inevitably prevailed!

I responded, "I don't want revenge, I just want what is right!" She gave me her classic Mona Lisa smile, which left me with little indication as to what she was about to say; but as usual, she did not disappoint me. In fact, her words still ring in my ears, and even today, when I deal with similar situations. "Robert," she said, "knowing the 'right thing' to do in life isn't always as easy as it seems. In this case, there are many other things to consider besides just making her pay, in whatever form, for what she has done. Look, she has been a good neighbor for more than twenty years, shouldn't that count for something?"

I held my ground: "Well, the least we can do is tell her that we know she stole our apples." Mother gave me a puzzled look. "But darling, why should we tell her what she already knows?"

What my mother had that I did not was experience in life. She knew that this woman was simply a human being who had made an error in judgment. From time to time, we all make wrong decisions. Even if she thought we might never uncover the truth, she would probably feel experience a much greater pain from her own conscience.

It was only a matter of two weeks before she came over to talk with my mother. It was obvious she wanted to confess, but Mother stopped her before she could explain. Placing her arm around the woman's shoulders in a comforting manner, she said, "Look, Louise, I can see you've been troubled over this unfortunate experience. You have been a wonderful neighbor and good friend for too many years to let this one incident change all of that. Let's forget it ever happened, and whenever you want apples for yourself and your family, you're always welcome to help yourself."

While I believe that compassion *is* my Mother's basic nature, her motives went much deeper. Her values and experience had taught her that forgiveness is far more practical than revenge. Although it took quite some time for our relationship with the neighbor to return to normal, it eventually did. In fact, it ultimately became much stronger and more meaningful.

Years later, I had the opportunity to revisit this lesson in a setting designed to uphold justice, but just the opposite occurred.

In the 1980's, there was an overabundance of competition inside the beltway, and many Washington, D.C. law firms were experiencing similar problems. One firm in particular was losing substantial market share and had begun to experience an erosion of its client base. Looking to take action to stop the bleeding and create a strategy for maintaining and growing their market share, the owners of the firm realized that what they needed was a sound marketing plan. At the time, marketing was a new concept to the legal profession.

As a public relations professional, I faced the inherent barriers that came along with that reality. The lawyers' perception of marketing was a euphemism for the unspeakable term, *selling.* It was considered the antithesis of what the profession had always represented to the public and its own self-image. I understood and sympathized with their concerns, but what further complicated matters was the fact that the firm suffered from the rivalries between departments and among associates that exist in every organization. It wasn't until I had been consulting with the firm for several months that I became a witness to an extreme example of their particular brand of rivalry.

On one side was a senior litigator who was successful and highly respected by the public and his peers. However, within his practice, he showed little patience or understanding to anyone who questioned his ideas and methods. He assumed absolute authority over his work and rarely delegated any of his responsibilities.

On the other side was his rival, a young, bright, ambitious attorney that questioned the logic behind employee policies. He was also a team player, who actively promoted shared participation and was not afraid to delegate responsibility. Their different personalities and management styles were mutually exclusive, and as a result, the two lawyers were on an inevitable collision course.

During my engagement with the firm, I witnessed a growing animosity between the two colleagues. The major source of irritation was the criteria used in determining voting rights and percentage of profit sharing for partners. The senior attorney argued that rights and shares should continue to be directly proportionate to tenure, while the junior attorney argued that an individual's performance should also be a consideration.

Partnership meetings became opportunities for relentless personal attacks. The other partners and associates went from being innocent bystanders to taking sides. The situation evolved into a 'we' older partners versus 'them' younger attorneys. In time, the office became a virtual battleground that only succeeded in tearing the basic fabric of the firm into pieces.

This situation made me think of Mother's question about revenge during the 'Case of the Missing Apples Caper.' During my daily activities at the firm, I frequently met with various departments and individuals. I was fortunate to have built a positive relationship with the younger attorney, revolving around the business plan and strategies for marketing the firm. As time passed, I felt I had 'earned-the-right' to begin a constructive dialogue with him concerning the conflict that had become a major distraction within the firm; resulting in a drop in overall productivity. After several weeks of general discussions, I asked him what he considered the root of the problem. He answered, "That's simple . . . they are one religion and we are another."

I asked whether he had ever given any thought to the ramifications of this on-going battle of wills. He paused for a long time and finally said, "It's been devastating, not only personally, but equally from the firm's point of view. It had reached to the point where something has to give, and that something will come down to a Waterloo for one of us. Our group believes our cause is just. It's a war of attrition, and I think we younger guys will eventually wear down the older guys."

"But at what price?" I asked. Having spent enough time with me to know that one of my mother's pearls of wisdom was not far behind, he said, "Okay Robert, let's hear it . . . what would your mother say in this situation?"

Smiling, I told him about the 'Missing Apple Caper.' I then followed with a detailed analysis of the current problem that involved taking himself out of the situation and adopting an objective, third-party point of view.

We discussed the 'Major Factors Affecting the Situation' and then labeled each one as either *'controllable,' 'uncontrollable,' 'positive,' 'negative,' or 'neither/or.'* The next step was to list all of the *inherent obstacles* he faced and then the *specific options* and appropriate *action steps.* After a lengthy study, he agreed that the best strategy was to accept the situation—as it was, and not as he perceived or thought, it should be. Next, he agreed to stop all direct or indirect confrontations that were not case related. He also agreed to show a greater degree of appropriate respect and cooperation. He also agreed to disband his group of loyal followers and advise them of the new strategy.

After a while, tensions began to lessen. Even his major adversary noticed. I asked the senior attorney how this affected his perceptions and thoughts concerning the issue. He replied that it had given him and the senior attorneys cause to reconsider the situation. As time passed, both sides were able to develop a much healthier and amenable relationship that led to a mutually acceptable compromise. The most interesting aspect of the problem is that attorneys train to resolve issues through negotiation, but as Mother often said, "In many cases, Robert, the plumber's house often leaks. They're so busy fixing other people's plumbing, they ignore their own." Truer words were never spoken.

My engagement with the firm ended, and I was packing up my belongings when the younger attorney happened to be passing by my temporary office. "Hey Robert, are you packing up to leave?"

I smiled and said, "All good things must come to an end. My job here is done, and it's time to move on." He thanked me for my support during those difficult times and mentioned that he felt that everyone benefited from the valuable lesson learned. Then he shared his own mother's advice. "My mother was an attorney, and she always said, 'The plumber's house often leaks. We're so busy fixing other people's plumbing; we forget to apply the same skills to our own problems.'"

"Your mother was a wise woman," I replied.

"Just one more thing Robert, I know our relationship with the senior partners will never be a love-fest, but that's okay," he said, adding, "We all have to learn to deal with what *is* and not we'd like it to be. If we had kept going on the same path, I had doubt it would have caused irreparable damage. I'm certain that in time, many of us would have left for greener pastures . . . but the grass isn't always greener on the other side."

In the end, we turned a potentially devastating situation into a promising one. I heard several months later that the firm was making steady progress in returning to their original purpose: the art of practicing law—*not revenge.*

FIRST IMPRESSIONS

Mother always said, "Robert, . . .
first impressions are like the first few steps in a race
—they can give you an early lead,
but the race isn't over until you cross the finish line."

IT WAS MY FIRST DATE. Boy, I was nervous just thinking about the fact that I was going out with one of the brightest, prettiest and most sought-after girls in my class; cheerleader Carol Mancini!

I was newly licensed, spit-shined and ready to go, but first I had to pass Mother's hygiene inspection: "Did you bathe, brush your teeth and shine your shoes?" *Check!* "Is your underwear clean; in case you're in an accident and have to go to the emergency room? I won't have my son caught dead in dirty underwear!" *Double check!*

Then she hit the critical issue—manners. "Remember to be polite and speak clearly when you introduce yourself to her parents. Nobody likes a weak-kneed boy—especially a girl! And most of all, show respect! Bring her home on time, or even better, a few minutes early. If you have any trouble, car or otherwise, call us immediately, no matter what time it is. Remember . . . on and on and on . . ." I was exhausted even before I left the house—it almost wasn't worth the date.

Mother's inquisition was so draining; I didn't have enough strength left to feel nervous.

There I was, pulling up in front of Carol's house. I parked the car and took a deep breath. As I walked up the steps, I could hear a loud thumping sound—like a bass drum—and it was coming from underneath my sports jacket! I had a sudden thought, *so this is why they call it a heartthrob* as I rang the doorbell. An older woman—Carol's grandmother—opened the door.

I walked into the living room, and Carol's parents—along with an overwhelming amount of religious artifacts prominently displayed on every table and adorning every wall—greeted me. As I introduced myself, I felt compelled to declare to Carol's parents that I was an altar boy for more than ten years; even as Mother's parting advice still echoed in my ears: "There are three things you never discuss: politics, family and religion—especially on the first date."

They offered a soft drink while I waited for Carol, who was still getting ready. I didn't realize it was common for the girl to be late, so that her parents could interview her date.

Carol's parents began the conversation, which reminded me of a little snowball that slowly starts rolling down a hill and eventually grows into an avalanche. It went something like this: "How long has your family been living in the area?" All of their lives—me included.

"How many brothers and sisters do you have?" I have one older brother who was recently elected president of his class. It never hurts to spread the wealth—value by association.

"Are your parents still living?" Yes—and they said to say, 'hello.'

They smiled approvingly. "What do your parents do for a living?" My father is a supervisor at J&L Steel mill, but three years ago, he was struck down by Tuberculosis and has been in the hospital ever since. Carol's grandmother compassionately chimed in with a heartfelt expression of concern. "I'll light a candle for him," she said, and I thanked her.

I told them about my mother; how she is a partner in the shoe business, and all of her customers love her so much, they won't let anyone else wait on them but her. I figured that endorsements would be a big plus when trying to impress a girl's parents.

Sensing the Q&A session was over, I thought a summary statement was in order, so I said, "I just want all of you to know, I think Carol is one of the nicest and smartest girls I have ever met." The look on their faces sent a clear message of approval. Not wanting to take anything for granted, I thought it would be a nice touch to add a safety record. "I've never received a speeding ticket, and I passed my driver's test on the first try. Oh, did I mention that I've made the honor roll the last three periods?"

Her parents were smiling from ear-to-ear, and Carol's grandmother clasped her hands together, looked up into the heavens and said in Italian,

"Grazie per questo bel ragazzo." I could only assume this was a positive, because when she finished, she came over and kissed me on the head. I found out later that it meant, thank you for such a nice boy. Lucky me!

Then, unexpectedly, the grandmother's face wore an expression of concern. Still on my best behavior, I asked if something was wrong. "Nothing's wrong, honey . . ." she said in a heavy Italian accent, "but I think you too skinny!" I told her it was hereditary, and she offered to feed me some homemade pasta, all the while saying that she was concerned that my slight build was not conducive for working in the vineyards. I thanked her and said, "I never thought of it that way." I learned later that this was her way of saying that she liked me.

Mother always said, "If you don't impress the grandparents and parents, it's not likely you're going to impress a girl." She was right. After almost an hour, Carol finally appeared, and it was worth the wait; she looked stunning! She apologized for being late and glanced at her parents and her grandmother in order to gain a sense of their feelings toward me. They all smiled, and realizing that I had just survived the crucial inquisition, I breathed a well-earned sigh of relief.

The rest of the night could not have been more perfect. After seeing a movie in the local theater, we went to the teen soda shop hangout. I returned her home safely, with fifteen minutes to spare. I thought about how I wanted to kiss her as we walked up the stairs and to the front door but I felt it might be premature on our first date. Just as I turned to leave, she tapped me on the shoulder and said, "I have something for you." She smiled, and then gave me a kiss on the cheek. It was kismet!

The next day, I called Carol, and she thanked me for the evening. She said she enjoyed herself, and—equally important—that her parents approved of me. Over the next year, love bloomed between us. Since we were approaching our first anniversary, I decided to ask a question, which had long been on my list of things to discover before I departed this Earth: "Why did you take so long to get ready on our first date?"

She laughed before explaining, "Well, it wasn't my idea, but my parents. They always want me to be intentionally late, so they can have a chance to talk to my date."

"We could have saved an hour," I replied, and Carol asked how. "They could have joined in my mother's pre-date checklist before I left home," I deadpanned.

Mother always placed a great deal of emphasis on making a *positive first impression*. Her definition of this went well beyond the traditional factors of dress, attitude and manners, which she saw as a mere reflection of a person's true character, beliefs and interests. According to my mother, the first impression sets the tone for what follows, and if the first impression is insincere, then the true character will eventually surface; in other words, people are caught in the act of being who they really are.

Whether consulting to a business or government, I recognized why my mother considered positive first impressions of such importance. She stressed that preparation was truly the key.

"Robert, if you know your audience's needs and expectations, then you're halfway there to making a sale," said Mother, further explaining that the reason she had such devoted shoe customers was based upon her knowing about their jobs, families, interests, favorite colors and styles and so much more . . . but without becoming involved in their personal lives.

"It's a fine line," she said, "and only time and experience can teach you how far to go. So, when in doubt, don't offer solutions—Just listen. People don't expect you to come up with solutions; they just want a warm and genuine *listener*."

I finally had the opportunity to test this early lesson in one of the most challenging situations I ever experienced in my career when a Fortune 500 company in New York City hired me to develop a long sought-after account.

I began my research by analyzing the company's history; including their goals, needs, supplier expectations, products, markets and competitors. In addition, I conducted an extensive investigation into the owner's nationality and cultural orientation. In order to gather information and gain different perspectives, I also interviewed some of my colleagues who called on them, as well. The major data I collected was as follows:

The Company—the fifth largest privately held supplier of textile goods in the world. Little public information was available, but reliable sources say they have little or no debt.

President—considered one of the most inscrutable but honorable men in the industry, he is of Turkish descent and known to be very religious. He rarely grants meetings with anyone outside of his inner circle. He is known as a fair but tough negotiator who contributes heavily to Middle Eastern health organizations and universities. The only known fact about his personal life is that all of his sons attended Harvard and held key positions within his company. His management style is direct and to the point, and he is very time-conscious. In addition, he is also known to place a heavy emphasis on moral and ethical values.

It took several months and the calling in of some favors just to schedule an appointment with him. Several days before the meeting, I focused on what I needed to do to make a positive first impression. I eventually decided that the best approach was to rely on the foundation of my basic principles in doing business, showing respect and common courtesies and trusting my instincts—no more and no less.

When the day of our meeting finally arrived, I entered his office building on Park Avenue feeling a degree of trepidation mix in with my excitement. Up in his office, the receptionist reminded me more of an executive assistant than her apparent function. The interior design was distinctively Middle Eastern, with original paintings and hand-woven tapestries hanging from every wall.

While waiting I had ample time to savor their originality and inherent beauty . . . at least two hours! Nevertheless, I knew that my being kept waiting was a test of my patience, not poor time management. Finally, I entered the inner sanctum of a textile industry legend. Surrounded by Middle Eastern-style opulence, and dressed in a finely woven white linen suit, Mehmet Nejat Ferit Eczacıbaşı was seated behind a massive mahogany desk, which had nothing on it but one large, ornate antique clock. A whirling white ceiling fan overhead reminded me of the one in my favorite movie, Casablanca.

Except for a string of 'worry beads,' which he deftly manipulated in his right hand, while appearing to be reading my mind. I remained standing, but I felt like a statue being assessed by a discriminating art collector as he seemed to be making the decision whether or not to 'buy' or 'dismiss' me. After what seemed like a millennium, he finally spoke.

His voice was a deep and raspy; similar to the great character actor, Sydney Greenstreet. He asked, "Why do you continue to stand, Mr. Popovich?"

I replied, "Because, Sir, you haven't yet given me permission to sit down." Expressionless, he nodded with approval.

Mehmet Nejat Ferit Eczacıbaşı then proceeded to give me a brief appraisal of my own nationality: "You are Serbian, Yes?"

I nodded, and he added, "They are hardworking people who stress honor, respect and education." I felt a sense of relief as he then began asking me questions about my heritage. Fortunately, knowledge about my ancestry was a prerequisite to maintaining a membership-in-good-standing within my family, so I passed his first test.

Next, he attempted to ascertain my general awareness of world politics, specifically the Middle East. I worked in Europe for over six years and frequently visited the Middle East for corporations and different governments, so I was able to offer my opinions on a variety of topics as they related to the textile industry. He listened, neither denying nor accepting my assessments.

I began feeling more comfortable until he asked what I considered a 'make or break' question: "Mr. Popovich, whom do you consider to be the villain in the Middle Eastern conflict?" My first reaction was, "This was the last question I wanted to be asked! It was then I remembered one of Mother's priceless gems: "If you ask a better question than was asked of you, you may have given an acceptable answer."

Carefully, I chose my words to acknowledge the weight and importance of his question, while avoiding placing judgment on any of the parties involved. "From whose perspective and to what end?" I asked him. My question elicited genuine surprise . . . and pleasure. Second test passed.

When he offered to introduce me to his sons, I felt honored and relieved. First he summoned his heir apparent and announced with obvious pride, "This is my oldest son; he will take my place one day."

After a brief exchange, he ordered this son to bring us tea. Then the second son appeared. We had barely shaken hands when he exited to assist his brother. The father apologized for the absence of his third son, explaining that he was in the Middle East doing business, while the youngest son was serving his apprenticeship by working at one of the company's distribution warehouses.

I found his treatment toward his sons was different than what I had expected, and he seemed to sense my reaction. "What do you think of my sons?" he asked me.

I replied, "I find them polite and respectful. I'm certain they represent you and your company honorably and competently." His immediate smile transformed into an intense expression of concern. "You know Robert, humility—like most human traits—isn't genetic; it must be taught and then earned." I agreed. Lesson understood; third test passed.

At this point, I felt reasonably comfortable, but I was nearing emotional exhaustion. He chose this moment finally to venture into my original reason for calling on him. "So, what can you tell me about my business that I don't already know?" he asked me.

"Until I have the opportunity to better understand your business goals and what challenges you might face, that's difficult to say," I answered, adding, "But based on my research, I would offer my assessment, and in those areas I feel my expertise may apply, I would make my recommendations." He concurred. Fourth test passed, with the finish line in sight!

However, Mother's voice played in my head: "Once the finish line is crossed, a new race is just beginning. And those who assume they have arrived usually fall victim to complacency." Then she would add, "Never forget that we are only as good as our last performance, and each new day we are back on the track, entering a new race in hopes of making another positive impression."

For good measure, she would add one of her favorite lines to remind me that first impressions only last if we remember to treat each subsequent impression as the first. "Ask yourself: 'I've been paid for yesterday, now what am I going to do for my company today?'"

PLANNING

Mother always said, "Robert . . .
if you don't know where you're going,
then how will you know when you've arrived?"

MOTHER WAS A FANATIC ABOUT PLANNING. Regardless of the size of the task, she always knew exactly *what* she wanted to achieve and *how*. I'll never forget one time when I was 12 years old: I'd been sitting on the back porch, looking forlorn, and when Mother asked what was wrong, I replied, "*nothing*," which always meant it was *something*. After the typical coaxing, I finally shared my frustration: I was losing money on my paper route and could not figure out why.

The route I inherited was from a good friend who had moved to Ohio. In the beginning, it was wonderful—75 long-time, steady-paying customers. All I had to do was deliver the papers and then collect approximately $20 every two weeks. Nevertheless, for some inexplicable reason, my profits started to drop—from $20 to $17 and then down to the unspeakably low sum of $12. I was devastated, and I could just see the headline: Paper Route Carrier Files for Bankruptcy

Mother started out by asking the obvious: "Robert, have you lost any customers recently?"

I replied, "Yes, but only a couple." Upon further reflection, I realized that what I thought was just "a couple," was actually ten, and those ten had been subscribed to the daily *and* the weekend edition! All of those subscriptions canceled were due to people moving out of the area, and I lost a net income of $5, but that did not explain the additional $3 loss. It turned out that this was attributable to the fact that 12 customers were receiving a special, introductory subscription rate.

"What's your plan for dealing with this situation?" Mother asked.

My objectivity was so clouded with self-pity; I figured I only had one choice. "I'll give up my paper route!" I declared, but that wasn't the answer she wanted or expected to hear.

"Nonsense," she replied. "You're not going to quit; you're going to make a plan!"

I gave her my patented *you've got to be kidding me* look and pointed out, "Mother, I'm just a kid! I'm not a business person!" She countered with her patented, *if you think, young man that you're just going to walk away from this job without giving it a chance; you're badly mistaken* look and again asked the obvious: "If you're not a business person, then what are you?" She pointed out that every business has a product, price, advertising and customers, and my paper route was just as much a business as any other business. "Okay," I conceded before lapsing into my former state of self-pity, "but I'm just a kid, what can I do?" I obviously needed a plan.

Mother quickly pointed out that the introductory subscriptions would eventually return to their normal subscription rates, and I would get back that extra $3. "But you need to figure out where you can earn that additional $5, and maybe even more," she added.

Suddenly inspired, I looked at her with great interest, "More?"

She smiled, and without an ounce of doubt replied, "Yes, much more; in fact, you have *two* ways to make more money. First, you should ask all of your daily customers if they'd be interested in subscribing to the weekend edition." She pointed out, "People's needs change, and unless you ask, you'll never know if you missed an opportunity."

Secondly, she said, I needed to find out whether any new families had moved into the neighborhood. I thought, *Wow! Why didn't* I *think of all of these great ideas?* Suddenly, I thought about a new housing development in the area that was under construction, and I realized that many new families would be moving in within the next six months. Boy, did I get excited! "Thanks, Mother, this is great stuff that will really help me! Are we done?"

"Not by a long shot," she answered, shaking her head. "You've fixed your immediate problem, but what about growing your business—what are your plans?" I just stared at her, mystified.

"Let me put it this way," she said, placing her hand on my shoulder, "don't you want to avoid having this problem in the future? Wouldn't you like to keep gaining customers and growing your paper route?"

I nodded, "Sure, but how?"

"You need a plan," she stated as she produced a sheet of paper and a pencil. She then told me to make a list all of my existing customers. "Check to see if they are happy with your delivery service," she advised. "Listen to what they say and then tell them to let you know if there's ever anything else you can do for them."

"That's such a great idea!" I exclaimed, thinking about all the ways I was going to gain customers and increase my profits and boy, was I *excited*!

Mother went on to say that, business is all about *common sense.* "Robert," she coached, "just remember what happened in the past, keep checking on the present, and then keep your ears to the ground on what's coming down the road, and you'll be in pretty good shape." She explained that customers always appreciate a job well-done, but they're even happier and more loyal if you constantly find ways to give them a little bit more than what they expect."

Thinking the woman was a genius, I asked her for an example. "Instead of throwing the paper on their walk, try putting it on their porch or in their mailbox," she said, adding, "I know you can come up with all sorts of ideas on your own, so I'll leave you to it.

The forlorn boy on the porch was transformed into an enthusiastic businessperson in just a matter of minutes! In addition, it was all because someone who was not emotionally involved in the situation was able to develop an actionable plan based upon the facts of the current situation. With this newfound information and inspiration, I envisioned a much different headline: Paper Route Carrier Has Record-Breaking Year

Years later, my mother's advice had brought me great success throughout my life, and I was now in a position to help *other* people fix their business problems.

One of the most memorable clients from my early years as a marketing consultant was a well respected, but financially troubled rehabilitation hospital in the Southwest United States. The year was 1985, and the hospital had an excellent staff, facility and reputation; however, their admissions numbers were dropping faster than barometric pressure during the hurricane season! In fact, business was so dismal that during one of my interviews with the hospital administrator, he confessed, "Robert . . . if I could just get up to 'broke,' I'd quit."

Shaking my head, I said, "That sounds pretty bad."

His voice quivered with urgency, as he looked me in the eye and said, "Look . . . if we don't turn this thing around in the next three months, we'll all be looking for work. So, even though I don't honestly think you'll make a difference, I thought we'd give it one last shot."

What a vote of confidence! With that attitude, I suspected that they would book me into the 'Last Resort Motor Inn.' I grinned at him and said, "Well . . . in that case, I hope I don't live up to your expectations." Then I started questioning this 'patient' about his organization's symptom.

After some deliberation, I determined the hospital suffered from a common but acute organizational illness—no marketing plan.

During the heyday of unlimited reimbursements and limited government intervention or oversight, the hospital flourished, so there wasn't a need for a marketing plan. In an effort to bring rising medical costs under control, the government imposed something called Diagnostically Related Guidelines, or DRG's, on all hospitals DRG's meant that there would be a maximum reimbursement for every medical procedure performed. The result of DRG's was stiffer competition between hospitals and a more educated and selective consumer. For this reason, the hospital's administration and staff needed to step back and analyze the hospital's new economic prognosis.

My research uncovered many interesting facts:

1. The public's perception of the hospital was that it was primarily a research center; not the excellent in-patient facility it now was.
2. Potential patients were unaware of the hospital's total service capabilities.
3. The hospital did not have a marketing department or plan.

The organization was in a death spiral, and it was my job to bring it back to life.

Along with the administration and department heads, I facilitated the development of a marketing plan, which outlined short—and long-term objectives, as well as marketing strategies, which would take advantage of the hospital's strengths and opportunities while reducing or even eliminating its weaknesses and threats in the marketplace.

In addition to helping them develop a strategy, it was my role was to provide the structure and design steps needed to implement the marketing effort. With renewed commitment, the medical staff, administration, and board of directors worked tirelessly to turn a hopeless situation into a promising future. After several months, the number of admissions steadily grew, enabling the hospital's new image to take hold in the marketplace. As an increasing number of patients took notice, the hospital regained its health and took its rightful place in the community.

Leaving the hospital for the last time, I first stopped by the administrator's office to bid him farewell. We briefly discussed the hospital's new marketing plan and its potential, and then he offered this assessment of his hospital's situation. "You know, Robert, when you're too close to the issue, it's difficult to keep things in proper perspective," he observed, and I agreed.

He added, "At times, gaining a fresh and different perspective can make a difference. I think the most interesting part about all of this is the fact that we were treating the symptoms rather than focusing on and identifying the actual illness. In this case, the right prescription turned out to be a marketing plan."

We shook hands, and I thanked him for the opportunity. "I look forward to seeing you once again, but hopefully under a different set of circumstances," I told him.

He smiled, patted me on the back, and said, "You can *plan* on it."

Mother used to say that planning could play a positive role in every aspect of our lives, not just in business. Therefore, whether you are considering a trip, a career, a relationship or an event, planning can save valuable time and money, as well as avoiding frustration. The key is to start with a specific objective that is measurable and attainable, as well as challenging.

According to Mother, rather than inadequate skills or limited resources, failures in life, or in business, are frequently the result of poor planning. She told me, "Robert, the easiest way to remember all that I've shared about planning is this: *plan your work, then work your plan,* and never to lose sight of your original goal, because without a final destination, how will you know when you've arrived?"

CURIOSITY

Mother always said, "Robert . . .
the only thing that is more predictable
than the need to eat,
is the need to discover."

I SPENT TWO WEEKS AT MY grandmother's house every summer. Each morning began with her homemade ***Palachinke,*** which is the Serbian version of crêpes. At midday, I would enjoy a bowl of her freshly churned ice cream. Special treats like these were topped off with a loosely enforced curfew that allowed me to hang out in her neighborhood, with the great group of my summer-time friends. No kid could ask for more!

We loved to play stickball on the street; amid the parked cars and proud row houses with their impeccably manicured yards, flower gardens, and porch swings. The rules were similar to baseball, but the equipment was makeshift—a tennis ball and a sawed-off broomstick.

As we played, we were always careful not to hit the ball into one particular yard; the creepy-looking Victorian-style house located at the far end of the street. Its broken blinds always drawn against filthy windows, the big, old house belonged to a recluse who scared even our parents. In fact, we were told in no uncertain terms, *never* to enter his yard.

The house's owner rarely, if ever, showed his face, but his rumored description was straight out of a horror flick—gnarled hands, scraggly beard, toothless mouth and always the same ragged clothes. No one knew much about his past or how he came to be so peculiar, but the biggest mystery was his name. For this reason, we dubbed him Mr. No Name that added to his mystique.

Unfortunately, his was the only part of the street usually free of parked cars. To make matters worse, the only time he ever appeared was when something landed on his property—most often our tennis ball.

Whenever an errant ball landed in his yard, he would spring into action; pushing opens his front door, running down the steps, and snatching the ball. At this point, he would stare menacingly at the guilty parties for a moment before quickly disappearing back inside his fortress. It was inevitable the next day; we found the ball cut into little pieces in the middle of the street. For this reason, those who hit the ball into Mr. No Name's yard *never* attempted to retrieve it.

On one particular day, my friend Tommy and I were playing stickball, and as luck would have it, the ball was hit into the out-of-bounds yard. When Mr. No Name failed to appear in his usual manner, I wondered aloud if he was even home. "Maybe we should go get it," I suggested to Tommy.

Tommy stared at me with disbelief before screeching, "ARE YOU CRAZY?" Even though my relentless badgering failed to change his mind, but unwilling to accept defeat, I resorted to the ultimate challenge: *I double-dog dared him.*

With that, he had no choice but to accept . . . or be humiliated.

We formulated the strategy, which was to enter the yard by climbing a fence that bordered the garage, hiding it from the house. Creeping alongside the garage wall until we reached the ball, we figured we were home free and decided to take the opportunity to peek inside Mr. No Name's garage. Raising ourselves slowly to the window, we peered inside, and a chill went up my spine upon spying a neatly aligned row of knives—ordered from the smallest to butcher knives—hanging on the far wall. Hypnotized, we rose up higher to see that below the knives was a row of perfectly aligned machetes.

Eyes wide with terror, we looked at each other briefly before returning to the windowpane, where we made our last discovery: a row of axes was leaning against the wall beneath the knives and machetes. Running through my mind—and probably Tommy's, too—was the burning question: *What does Mr. No Name cut up besides tennis balls?*

For some unfathomable reason, Tommy's curiosity got the best of him, and he suggested we peek into one of the windows in the house. I didn't think it was such a good idea, but he was relentless, resorting to the highest challenge a child could ever face. He grabbed both of my shoulders, looked me straight in the eye and said, *"I triple-dog dare you!"* I stared back at him, defeated. With that matter settled, we crept forward.

Staying low, I held my breath and was not even aware of it as we shimmied against the house in the direction of the kitchen window.

Rising up tiptoe to look inside, I suddenly felt a strong hand grip my shoulder, and out of the corner of my eye, I saw another hand clamp down on Tommy's shoulder, too. In a deep, gravelly voice, the old man growled, "What are you kids doing in my yard!" Figuring this was a rhetorical question, we both began screaming as we ripped ourselves free of his grasp and started racing toward the fence. Approximately three feet high, we had we climbed over it on our way into his yard, but thanks the adrenaline that raced through our veins, we leaped over it like Jesse Owens clearing hurdles at the Berlin Olympic Games.

That night, I couldn't sleep. Plagued with fears that Mr. No Name would slip into my bedroom to exact his revenge; I trembled beneath the covers until dawn. Fortunately, Mother arrived the next morning to pick me up, and I was more than ready to leave. Right away, she noticed my unusual sense of urgency to leave Grandma's house and began her interrogation.

As soon as she had extracted the truth from me, she demanded that I go and apologize to Mr. No Name, but then she reversed her decision. Sensing my fear and seeing my remorse, she stated, "All right, you don't have to apologize, but remember; it's okay to be curious, but *not* when you've been told otherwise." I could not have agreed more.

Years later, I experienced a similar situation, but this time the roles were reversed. One of my co-workers had an insatiable appetite for gossip. In fact, I often thought that his behavior was comparable to that of chickens searching for food in a yard: their heads jerking and bobbing in all directions.

Jerry, our chicken, would always enter my office wearing a big smile. "Hi, Robert, any new tantalizing tidbits you can share?" he would inquire, all the while focusing his eyes on my desk in his quest for juicy information. In fact, I once stepped out of my office for a few moments and returned to find him leafing through and reading the papers on my desk. As he called on excuses that ranged from needing a pencil and paper to write a note to wanting to tidy up my desk, I finally reached my limit with this man, but

I realized that confronting him would be constructive. So, my first step was to set an objective: How can I stop Jerry's behavior without hurting his feelings? It was a worthwhile challenge.

The next time he arrived in my office on one of his usual reconnaissance patrols, he walked into a trap. While talking with him, I grabbed a document and slowly turned it over, knowing he would watch intently. Appearing nervous, I said to him, "Oh! Did you know the company picnic date has been changed?" but he didn't hear a word I said. He was too busy looking at that piece of paper. Ignoring the paper, I continued the conversation and then asked him if he wouldn't mind taking telephone messages, while I stepped out for a moment. Of course, he was more than willing.

"Yes! I'd be glad to!" he answered, grinning widely. I left the room knowing that he would probably pick up the memorandum and read it right away. What *he* didn't know was that I had written GOTCHA in big, bold letters on the other side.

When I returned, I thanked him for watching my phone, and I noticed that his expression contained a mixture of embarrassment and disappointment. I asked Jerry if he had taken any messages for me, and his reply was a barely audible "No" before he added, "Well . . . I'd better be going."

After this, he stayed away from my office for several days. When he did return, we exchanged our usual pleasantries, but I wasn't prepared for what came next: "Remember the other day when you asked me to watch your phone?" he asked, and I nodded, feeling a deep sense of regret. Then his face softened and a warm smile followed. "I guess you got me," he admitted, "hook, line, and sinker!" Without warning, we both started laughing hysterically.

In the event you're *curious*, Jerry's snooping did end. It seems my little trap forced him to recognize that had he continued his ways, the consequences might have been much worse. As a result, our friendship and mutual respect took on a new, positive dimension.

ANXIETY

Mother always said, "Robert, . . .
nothing is ever as good as it seems
—or as bad as it seems, so relax and
deal with life's challenges one step at a time."

WHENEVER MY MOTHER WOULD SAY, "Robert, we need to have a little talk," I would instinctively respond with, "Why? Did I do something wrong?" My heart sank, because in the past it meant I was in some kind of trouble.

From birth to death, stress is a part of life; an experience very few get to avoid. Assuming something is wrong before knowing all the facts is a big cause of anxiety, but my mother's advice about assumption was down-to-earth: Even if you're facing a negative situation, don't put yourself at a disadvantage before you have all the facts. "Wait and see how things develop," she advised, "and then goes from there." It was sound, logical advice, but sometimes difficult to follow.

For instance, any child summoned to the principal's office at school knows the feeling of high anxiety.

I will never forget sitting in my sixth-grade math class when an ominous knock at the classroom door made everyone's blood run cold. A messenger then handed the teacher a slip of paper, and we all heard her say, "I'll get him for you." Our class was equally divided—fifteen boys and fifteen girls—so we knew the girls were off the hook.

Meanwhile, the boys were practicing that age-old art of appearing indifferent by looking casually out the window, all the while reviewing in their minds any recent misconduct and possible punishments. When the teacher announced, "Robert, you are wanted in the principal's office," the rest of the boys heaved a collective sigh of relief.

My immediate reaction was to think that someone must have died in my family. Then, I considered that I might be in serious trouble. Either way, both possibilities were equally unattractive.

I glanced around the room for some sign of support, but I only received blank stares. I tried to stand up, but I felt nailed to the chair. It was my first experience of total mental and physical impairment caused by acute paranoia. After a few moments, I was able to stand up, but my legs were shaky, eliciting whispers and stares from the rest of my class as I awkwardly made my way out of the room.

When I arrived at the principal's office, his secretary greeted me. "Yes, how may I be of assistance?" she asked, impatiently.

Feeling my throat start to close, I squeaked, "I was told to report to the principal's office."

She offered me a seat and returned to her duties. Five minutes passed, then ten, and as they ticked by, my anxiety began to rise. By the time I entered his office, sweat was running down my face, my hands were shaking, and my heart was racing.

Upon my entrance into his inner sanctum, the principal stood up and came around his desk to greet me with a friendly smile and warm hand on my shoulder. This pleasant reception immediately quelled my anxiety.

When asked if I knew why he wanted to see me, I said I had no idea. "I know your family celebrates Eastern Orthodox Christmas on January 7th," he explained, adding that he just wanted to extend his holiday greetings to my family and me.

Dramatically wiping the sweat from my brow, I thanked him before politely suggesting that in the future, he consider using Western Union. He laughed appreciably.

When I arrived home that day, I shared the experience with my mother, and she asked, "So, what did you learn from this ordeal?"

I quipped, "To always take a bottle of Pepto-Bismol in my lunch bag." She just shook her head. "That's not exactly what I meant," she said. "Oh, you always say not to jump to conclusions until you have all of the facts. Well, that's easy to say, but sometimes it's very hard to do," I told her.

"That's true," she agreed, "however, the more we practice anything, the easier it becomes. In time, you'll learn that it can save you from having a nervous breakdown; and you won't have to carry around a bottle of Pepto-Bismol." I eventually came to realize how right she was.

Throughout our lives, we all learn that anxiety comes in different forms, levels of intensity and impact in our lives. Early in my career, I experienced the most severe type of anxiety when I became an unwitting victim of circumstances that not only resulted in my loss of personal freedom, but also threatened my life.

In November of 1979, I was on my way to the Middle East to attend a conference in Kabul, Afghanistan. I eagerly looked forward to being introduced to a unique, and most might say, inscrutable culture, but I could not have guessed that it would exceed my expectations . . . in the worst possible way.

The US State Department routinely offers safety travel advisories for US citizens, so that they may make informed decisions when traveling to high-risk regions of the world. I was aware that the Middle East was a historic hotbed of political and religious strife, but I naively did not believe that those warnings applied to me; and why should they? I was just another businessperson going on a normal business trip . . . or so I thought.

The journey began uneventfully in New York. The first stop was London, then Frankfurt, followed by Rome. Seated beside me during the entire trip was the Israeli ambassador to the United Nations. I felt fortunate to have him as a traveling companion. His experiences were a fascinating history lesson in international affairs. After Rome, our next stop was Istanbul, Turkey, followed by our last refueling stop in Tehran, Iran, before going on to our last destination—Kabul, Afghanistan.

As we neared Iranian air space, the Pan American Airlines captain suddenly announced on the public address system that we were heading into a crisis. "If you look out on either side of the aircraft," he told us, "you'll see large plumes of smoke encircling the entire perimeter of the airport." We had unfortunately arrived in the middle and height of the Iranian Revolution. The captain further explained that a number of different separatist factions were fighting for control of the government, and the airport was of strategic importance. Given the gravity of the situation, we were not permitted to taxi to the main terminal, instead we were taken to a remote part of the airport. Once there, guards boarded the plane and collected everyone's passports. We were forced to remain sweltering aircraft without explanation, apology, or air-conditioning for hours.

When they finally gave us permission to deplane, they ordered us inside an enormous Quonset hut that housed military aircraft and weaponry. Once inside, the guards asked everyone the same questions regarding whether or not we had an entry visa, our final destination and the purpose of our trip. Being one of more than 300 passengers gave me a sense of security, until they separated ambassador and me from the group. Then, they took him to one interrogation room and me to another, and I never saw him again.

When they asked for my visa, I explained that there hadn't been enough time for one to be issued before I left the United States, but I was promised that it would be waiting for me once I arrived in Kabul; unfortunately, it hadn't. To make matters even worse, their suspicions mounted as they took note of the unusually high number of customs stamps in my passport and factored in that I was an American. Their inability to speak English or any other major European language just compounded the situation.

For the next four hours, I sat nervously waiting in the interrogation room until an officer who spoke a modest number of English could be located. Displaying limited interest or concern, he asked me the same questions, over and over again. I kept repeating the same answers, until my fear slowly turned into a quiet rage.

When the interrogation ended, three armed guards escorted me to a waiting military vehicle. They denied my persistent requests to speak with someone from the US Consulate and confiscated all of my personal belongings, passport, except for my toiletries.

They transported me to a remote site, roughly three hours away from the city; held captive for several weeks, without an explanation or contact with the outside world. Each passing day left worse or me with little hope, that I would be released. With little to eat or drink, I lost an appreciable amount of weight that left me with little physical and emotional strength to endure daily draining interrogations. Their objective was simple, admit to being a CIA operative spying for the—as they put it—American infidels. To everyone back home—my family, my company, my government—I had essentially dropped off the face of the earth, and with each passing day, left them little hope that I was alive.

Throughout this ordeal, I kept reminding myself of Mother's adage that *nothing is ever as good . . . or as bad as it seems,* although I never anticipated this type of experience to test its merits. I was confident, however, that any research they employed would confirm that I was not a real or potential threat. Then on the thirtieth day of my confinement, and without reason or apology, they returned my passport, and drove me directly to the airport with explicitly instructed me to never return; and if I did, it would result in imprisonment or possibly worse.

I boarded the next flight to London, and once safely in the air, I reflected upon the seriousness of my situation, and possible consequences. I thought how little control we have over many events in our lives and how ill prepared we often are to deal with extreme and unexpected situations. I realized how fortunate I was to live in a free society.

Anxiety can be self-induced or others can cause it. In either case, it is the mental attitude we bring to every situation that can greatly influence its outcome, especially during seemingly hopeless circumstances. I believe it is important to maintain control over our emotional reactions and deal with worrisome issues one-step at a time. To do otherwise can place us in an undesirable position or at an unnecessary disadvantage. As Mother always said, *"Nothing is ever as . . ."*

JEALOUSY

Mother always said, "Robert . . .
if you can turn your enemy into an ally
—you will never have a greater ally."

EVERY HOLIDAY SEASON, MOTHER TOOK us on our Christmas excursion into the city. The festive department store windows beckoned us as we shopped for family gifts, as well as new holiday outfits for my brother Charles and me. Three years older and many inches taller, my brother understandably received more clothes than I did, since I could inherit his hand-me-downs. This fact never came to light, until the year, I realized that our clothing tastes were as different as our personalities.

I was almost 13 years old and beginning to feel my first conscious pangs of self-pity and jealousy. Sensing my distress, Mother quietly asked, "What's wrong, Robert? You're usually very excited about our trip to the city."

With my head hung low, I sullenly answered, "I guess I'm just growing up." She didn't press the issue, and we left it at that, but it was clear that there was a battle on the horizon.

Mother often said the timing determines the outcome of a conflict. In this instance, she chose to delay the inevitable confrontation.

I went to my room and began dwelling on one of my favorite themes: the gross injustice of being the youngest sibling. My brother's achievements were meteoric—an honors student was a student council representative and officer, member of the marching band and considered one of the most quick-witted, popular members of his class and good athlete.

Charles was so memorable that people frequently called me by *his* name. Thus, I felt that I was a victim of a double whammy—always a half step behind his achievements, with little or no identity of my own. His bar was often too high for me to reach, and that drove me crazy, but the fact that my brother was always supportive and caring drove me insane!

Later that evening, Mother came to my room and sat down beside me on my bed. Gently, she smoothed the hair on top of my head and softly said, "So, what seems to be troubling you?" Proudly, dishonestly I proclaimed, "Nothing!" She didn't respond. She just sat there quietly and waited.

When my frustration eventually broke free of my faltering grasp, I sobbed, "It's so unfair being the youngest in the family! Especially when you have a brother who's so much better than you at *everything*."

Instead of listing the reasons why I should not think that way, she said, "Did you know that *I* was the third oldest child in my family of nine? Can you imagine what *that* was like?" She told me how every morning was a circus of siblings, all trying to get ready for the day with only one bathroom. She pointed out that each child in the family yearned for special attention from their parents.

Mother gently coaxed me out of my mood with tales of what it was like to be part of a very large family. "That must have been wild," I told her my respect for her growing appreciably as I imagined having to compete with so many brothers and sisters.

"It was," she agreed, "but somehow, it all seemed to work out." "How?" I wondered.

"First, we loved one another very much; family came before all else," she explained. "Second, my parents tried to give each of us equal attention and whatever things we needed, but that was not always possible. Would you believe we had to share everything at least three times?"

"Like hand-me-downs?" I asked.

"Exactly," she replied.

I asked her what it was like to grow up in the shadow of others, and she laughed. "We had so many in our family that the shadow was more like a lunar eclipse!" she said. "You have to understand and accept the fact that life isn't always going to be as fair as we would like it to be. However, for every *dis*advantage, there always seems to be an *ad*vantage, and vice-versa."

She often said, *the mind must be tilled, as a field, before good seeds are planted."* In that spirit, she started digging with a question. "Tell me, Robert, what do you think are the advantages of being the youngest?" I looked at her with obvious skepticism, so she started digging with a bigger, and more thought provoking questions.

"For example, who is responsible for watching you when we're not at home?"

"My brother," I answered.

"Who plays ball with you every day and includes you in his group of personal friends?"

"My brother," I repeated, starting to notice a trend.

"Who's the first to defend you when we want to take away privileges for misbehaving?" she continued.

I just looked at her, as my argument as my argument quickly faded. She went on to dig the hole even deeper. "And who do we expect to set the perfect example of behavior for his younger brother?"

"I get the point!" I groaned.

She looked at me tenderly. "I'm not telling you these things to make you feel guilty or imply that your brother is perfect, because he isn't; but who is? Whenever you're feeling upset about what you think is unfair, remember that there is always another side to the story."

Once again, the sage had pulled me from the adolescent flames of self-pity and placed me safely into the hands of a developing maturity. As the years passed, so did many of my feelings of inadequacy and anonymity.

With growing maturity, we learn that comparisons have no bearing on how well we perform or how others perceive us. In the final analysis, each one of us must stand alone when determining our worth. To think otherwise will only become a debilitating and unnecessary distraction. However, a small amount of constructive sibling rivalry is not without its rewards.

There was one way in which I outdid my brother: I grew to be two-and-a-half inches taller, However, I am the first to admit that he stands tall in every way. In fact, his lifelong devotion to education has carried him to a professorship at a highly respected university. In time, I came to realize that he was, and continues to be, one of my most devoted allies.

I am convinced that the insidious seeds of jealousy never die. They may lie dormant in our minds over time, but jealousy stands ready to sprout with little or no warning, often without reasonable logic.

My Aunt Mary, my mother's older sister tells a wonderful story about a jealous colleague that best illustrates this point. Actively involved in politics for many years, my aunt was one of the leading political figures in Pennsylvania. In fact, during the Carter Administration, she frequently visited the White House to consult with the president.

Despite her political stature, she never boasted or even considered her prestigious assignments as anything other than a normal part of her job. On the other hand, her New York City counterpart; also a senior Democratic delegate from her district, regularly measured her own success and degree of influence against my aunt's accomplishments and contacts.

This woman had a burning desire to attend a luncheon with the president. Eventually, she received an invitation to attend an "intimate" White House luncheon with approximately 200 other delegates; she could not wait to share the news with my aunt.

Several weeks later, they were attending another delegate luncheon when the New Yorker spied my aunt, seated with ten other prominent women. Prancing up to the seated delegates, she loudly called, "Good afternoon, ladies!" with her unmistakable Queens accent. Then she added, "And you, too, Mary. Guess who I had lunch with the other day?"

No one reacted. Undeterred, the woman stood at attention with her shoulders pulled firmly back, her eyes glowing with pride. "The President of the United States of America!" she declared with fervor. For a brief moment, my aunt recalled, everyone expected her to begin singing the Star Spangled Banner.

"That's great! How was it?" Aunt Mary asked her. "It was won-der-ful, if you know what I mean," the woman gushed. "The president gave such a rousing speech that he received a standing ovulation!"

Calmly Aunt Mary replied, "Well, that is impressive!"

There was a brief moment of silence before all of the women at the table broke into raucous laughter, causing them to make some unflattering comments about this woman who had unwittingly turned herself into a joke. My aunt, however, recognized it as an opportunity to gain a potential convert.

She quickly took the mortified woman aside and said with genuine sensitivity "Look, this is no big deal; we've all had our moments of embarrassment." After that, the two continued their conversation about the New Yorker's White House experience and the incident served to build a solid foundation and a more congenial relationship. In another expression of goodwill, my aunt let the New Yorker take her place at another White House function that following week. The woman was overwhelmed with gratitude and appreciation. Aunt Mary had won her over with these acts of kindness, forging a *real* friendship, and proving my aunt's favorite maxim: *Take an enemy and turn them into an ally, you will never have a greater ally.*

INTELLIGENCE

Mother always said, "Robert . . .
asking good question, is like eating a lot of fish
—they both develop great minds."

IT WAS DINNER TIME, AND Mother sat expressionless as she reviewed my final grades from my first year in college. Her eyes moved slowly across the paper, as she carefully examined my marks, and after what seemed like a millennium, she finally spoke. "Congratulations!" she said, her smile glowing with pride. "Your grades are wonderful! And just think—next year you'll be a *sophomore*."

Later that evening, as I helped her clear the dinner table, I began pondering the anomaly of a woman with little education whose intelligence I would match against anyone. Wondering about her formula for success, I said, "Mother, I have a question."

"Good," she replied.

I wondered why she answered that way. Why didn't she just say *yes*?

"Because, *yes,* doesn't tell you how important I think questions are," was her reply. She recalled an old adage her father often repeated, *"Asking good questions is like eating a lot of fish—they both develop great minds."*

At that moment, I came to the realization that throughout my life, my mother has been a human questioning machine. I had to ask, *"Why?"* "Mother, why are you always asking questions?" I probed.

She didn't hesitate. "Well, not having a formal education, I knew I had to assume the responsibility for educating myself, and there was only one way to do that—by reading everything I could lay my hands on and learning from my experiences," she explained, but she could tell from the dour expression on my face that I was unconvinced.

She was up to the challenge. "You know how when someone in school asks a lot of questions, they're labeled a brown noser or a bookworm?" I nodded. "It was that way even when I was in school, but you have to look beyond what children say; because their opinions won't count once you're out in the world, and you have to make a living."

Not wanting to dwell on the whole bookworm thing, I asked her to lay out the basics for me: "How do you know what questions to ask?"

She paused a moment before saying, "My general rule of thumb is this: Just ask those questions that are necessary to satisfy your needs at a given time." She went on to explain that people don't usually mind answering questions, as long as they feel you are interested and your questions have relevance.

"You should always have a goal when you ask questions," she advised. "For example, when I used to ask my boss about the store inventory, I had a specific purpose in mind: *Do we have enough shoes in stock to meet customer demand?"*

Then she added a warning: "Never ask more questions than you can handle. It's the same principle I teach you when you sit down to eat: Only take as much as you can finish, then if you're still hungry, you can always go back for more. It's the same with learning."

Satisfied, I confessed, "I used to get so irritated when you would answer my questions with another question, but now I understand why. Your questions made me think and then justify my views when dealing with issues—all the while keeping my emotions in proper perspective. In addition, I usually remembered the lesson much longer," I said before adding, "It's strange, but the older I get, the smarter you become." For once, she didn't respond with a question. She just looked at me in a way that made me know that *she* knew I was getting it. Her lessons were finally sinking in.

Her approach became an active part of every phase of my personal and business development. It was particularly useful in a city that thrives on answering questions with questions: New York City, New York.

The fashion district on NYC's West Side is a country in and of itself. Watching daily activities on the street and in the buildings can't help but remind me of one of the most studied and intelligent societies known to science: *an ant colony*. At first glance, the ants appear to be scurrying about with little purpose. When put under the microscope, however, we discover an ant colony is a finely tuned organization; geared for efficiency with the overriding objective of survival.

Even though it runs at a hectic pace, the fashion industry is organized for maximum productivity. My involvement in the West Side ant colony was to represent one of the largest textile manufacturers in the country. I called on major distributors in hopes of placing my client's goods in their lines. The job became especially enjoyable after I had built up a strong rapport and mutual respect with the distributors.

Typical sales calls always gave me the feeling of being in an echo chamber. I would ask the question that frequently begins many New York conversations, "So, how's business?"

The usual response went like this: "How should it be? Are you writing a book, or what?"

I would persist with, "Really, how is it going?"

Response: "So, you really want to know?"

Then I would nod, and in what approached a lament, I would hear something like this: "You should have such pain! I wouldn't wish today's market on my worst enemy, unless of course he was my major competitor."

This seemingly meaningless colloquial bantering served two important purposes. First, it was a tradition; and second, it served as a positioning tool before the hard negotiations got underway.

One of my favorite experiences was with Izzie Carten, a very successful global mover of goods; but if you visited him in his warehouse, you would not believe it. His warehouse was located in one of the worst sections of the lower East Side. The massive double entry, garage-style doors that led to his particular anthill were made of solid steel. When you knocked on them, he opened a sliding peephole to ensure you were not *persona non grata.* Once granted entry, a short, stout, balding, unshaven man chewing on an unlit cigar, dressed in tattered clothes, sporting a voice that challenged the annoyance of fingernails scraping on a chalkboard, greeted you. It confirms the adage, *never judge a multi-millionaire by his cover.*

Izzie Carten's warehouse was at least three football fields long, with bolts of cloth stacked on shelving as high as the Empire State Building. The eerie part about this scene was the fact that we were alone. When we spoke, our voices reverberated like echoes in a canyon; and the place had the look and feel of a real-life chamber of horrors. I could only assume that the movement of goods happened under the shroud of darkness, but I never had good reason to ask. There are times when some things are better left unsaid.

This strange, little man had the horrible habit of wrapping scotch tape around his last three fingers, making them turn blue due to the loss of circulation. Why he did, this was anyone's guess, but then again, some mysteries don't need to be revealed.

I called on him for more than three years, and our encounters always followed the same script: He asked the same questions, and I gave him the same answers. It was not so much a game as a means to either wearing down my position or assessing if there had been any changes in the pricing policy of the company I represented. His initial remarks revolved around how tough business was and how much his costs had risen. I routinely acknowledged his points, without necessarily agreeing. He would then ask me to show him the prices on staple goods from which he reaped consistently high profit margins. His philosophy was *more is always better.*

However, that didn't deter him from trying to bargain for a better deal. His standard line was, "So, Robert, what are you going to do for me this year on price?"

I would smile and say, "The same thing I did for you last year: a fair price that will still meet both of our profit-margin objectives."

He always countered with, "You know, business is tough. You try and keep two kids in Harvard, a house in the Hamptons, and one on Martha's Vineyard, two maids, and a driver. It's not easy!" My immediate reaction was to laugh, but I quickly stifled the impulse, reminding myself that everything in life is relative.

Instead, I answered his complaint with a question: "What do you think might happen if I gave you a lower price?"

"You'd make me happy," he replied, simply.

"True, but don't you think I'd have to offer the same price to my other customers?" I pointed out, but that answer didn't satisfy him.

"Maybe so," he persisted, "but you represent one of the largest textile manufacturers in the business. You should be able to do better than the others—right?"

I shrugged. "Maybe, but let me ask you a question: What's the biggest reason you do so much business with us?"

I watched as his eyebrows went up. "That's easy," he answered, "the quality of your goods."

I continued, "And what do you think might suffer the most if we began lowering our prices to be more cost-competitive?"

His lips pursed together, and he started to stammer. "Well . . . you have a point, but . . ."

I followed with, "Lower prices would be nice, but what might be the ultimate cost?"

He thought for a long moment, and then finally conceded. "I might not be able to do the volume of business I'm presently doing if the quality begins to slip," he admitted. Then he reached into his back pocket, pulled out a white handkerchief and began waving it. "I surrender!" he cried, his grin wide. "But it never hurts to ask."

We both burst out laughing, and he subsequently placed another big order for our goods before and I had the pleasure of taking him to lunch—as per tradition.

Stating as opposed to *asking* may save time, but Mother's advice was always to ask. Experience had convinced her that a properly phrased question could be a game-changer—frequently in your favor. She believed a question could have a greater influence and staying power than most statements of fact.

I've learned that a good question can reduce tension, set the stage for a productive conversation and, more importantly, educate through one of the least expensive, but priceless methods; learning from the experience of others.

HUMILITY

Mother always said, "Robert . . .
there is no one more important than you;
and remember, there is no one less than you."

IF THERE IS ONE QUALITY, my mother considered at the top of her list—it was humility. She looked beyond its obvious benefit of reducing the amount of verbal fertilizer in the world. She considered it, if not the most important; certainly one of the most important traits a person needs in order to achieve happiness and success in life.

"Humility," she insisted, "is as important as the air we breathe. Without it, we will suffocate on our own and other's praise."

Whenever she sensed the slightest nuance of, *I'm-so-important-just-ask-me* syndrome going on with me, she shared one of her favorite bedtime stories. Throughout the years, I often needed a refresher, so I know this one by heart. It always went like this:

"Come here dear, and sit beside me, I want to tell you one of my favorite bedtime stories," she would say as she positioned herself at the head of my bed. In her softest voice, she began with the usual fairy-tale opening; "Once upon a time, in a faraway land, there lived a little boy who was the apple of his mother's eye. She taught him that even the most perfect apple could become spoiled if it listened to the big, ugly, slimy, green, two-headed monster: Mr. Look-at-Me! And, Mr. Listen-to-Me!

"One day, the little boy was just minding his own business when the monster appeared and told him that he was the biggest, brightest, and most beloved apple in the orchard. Every day, the monster would whisper accolades in the little boy's ear about how wonderful and delicious he was . . . how he was *so* much better than all the other apples. After some time, he came to believe that what the monster said was true; he discovered that none of the other apples wanted anything to do with him anymore, because it only takes one rotten apple to spoil a whole bunch of good apples. Fearing for their lives, they cut his stem, and he toppled to the ground; left alone with no one noticing or caring."

I was full of remorse. "Oh Mother," I gasped, "That's just awful! What happened to him? Why didn't anyone try to help him?"

She always reassured me; "Someone did try to help him. It was his mother. She baked him her favorite, most delicious recipe for Humble Pie, and when he finished eating it, he immediately turned back into the precious *apple of her eye,* and they lived happily ever after!"

At that point, I breathed a sigh of relief . . . until I realized that she was talking about *me*. Humbly, I said, "I think you've make your point!" smiling apologetically.

"Good," she said, always softening my sense of humiliation and regret for how I had acted with a treat. The last time I needed to hear her bedtime story, my surprise was a promise to take me out to wherever I wanted to celebrate my birthday. That was the year I turned 25.

There are times when a refresher course on humility is in order. I recall one occasion when I had returned home after spending an extended amount of time in Europe, dealing with my many clients there. Traveling and long absences from home are part of my business.

Whenever I return, it's customary to enjoy my family's company over dinner, and expected to give Mother a full update on my recent adventures.

Well, one Thanksgiving, as our family of four sat surrounding a large bird that was appropriately dressed for the occasion, the focus of the discussion was on my brother's latest meteoric professorial academic achievement.

My mother brought up one of his more recent awards. Charles nodded in appreciation, but still remained silent. "Just think, Robert, your brother is only the second professor in the school's history to receive this prestigious research award," Mother pointed out.

Sitting beside him, I patted him on the back. "Great!" I exclaimed. "You must be in Seventh Heaven." As it turns out, this wasn't far from the truth, as evidenced in the way he displayed his unmistakable, *'Awww, shucks! Twern't nothing'* look.

"We're all so proud!" said Mother, glowing. "In fact, he'll receive the award at the dean's residence with only a few faculty dignitaries invited."

By now, my brother's chest was rising faster than a weather balloon. His usual controlled manner quickly transformed into a Burning Bush of egotistical illumination while he feigned modesty. It was quite obvious to those of us who knew him well that he was quite pleased with himself.

"Tell us, Charles," she prodded, "how does it feel to be at the receiving end of such a prestigious award?"

He sat up in his chair, cleared his throat, looked around the table and offered his thoughts: "It was nothing, really," he humbly countered, "It's just a part of what we do as professors. It is expected; although, I must admit, it did challenge every aspect of my intellectual capacity. At the end of the day, I think the award speaks for itself." Or did it? He had a captive audience, and he took advantage of it.

I politely listened; my father dozed off, and my mother's eyes signaled her growing impatience, so she took control of the conversation. "Excuse me, dear," she injected. "No offense, but are you aware that thirty minutes have passed since you told us that *the award speaks for itself?"*

His eyes suddenly widened in disbelief, but at the same time, he somehow managed to regain his composure. "I did?" he questioned. "Are you certain? That's impossible!" He stopped talking when he noticed me, pointing at my wristwatch.

"Yes, my brother, you did!" I verified, and everyone started laughing, with my brother laughing the loudest. I turned to my mother. "Apparently, Mother, you never told my brother the story about the big, ugly, slimy, green, two-headed monster: *Mr. Look-at-Me* and *Mr. Listen-to-Me*." My brother had no idea what we were talking about, so my mother decided that this was the perfect time to share her bedtime story with him.

"Robert, why don't you and your father go into the living room . . . we'll be over in a minute," she told us. As we left the room the last words I heard her say were, "Charles, please come over here and sit down next to me, I have a wonderful story to share with you."

The startled look on his face was priceless. Once she finished telling him the story, they joined us in the living room for coffee, and, of course, each one of us received a large slice of her incomparable *Humble Pie.*

PERSUASION

Mother always said, "Robert . . .
the easier you make it for me to buy
—it is more likely that I will."

IF PEOPLE HAD TO CHOOSE BETWEEN one skill above all else, it might very well be the ability to persuade. Most everything in our lives depends upon convincing others to believe in us. Throughout my life, I marveled at my mother's ability to do just that, and the most amazing aspect of her ability was, she made it look effortless.

I attributed her talent to God . . . accompanied by her years of experience, both as a parent and as a businesswoman.

I vividly remember the moment when I came of age—wanting to know her secrets of persuasion.

I dubbed this life-changing moment The Opposing Forces of Nature. On one side was my father—the Immovable Object, and on the other was my mother—the Irresistible Force. On the surface, it would appear to be a stalemate, but things are rarely as they appear. My mother, brother and I wanted to take a mini-long weekend holiday in Niagara Falls; however, my father wanted to stay home.

The significant difference between my mother's and my father's likelihood of success was my mother's higher level of determination, confidence, enthusiasm, and preparedness. Other than those factors, it was an even match.

The long holiday weekend was nearing, and Mother saw it as the perfect opportunity for our family to get away and recharge our batteries; unfortunately, my father was diametrically opposed to the suggestion. He considered that weekend as the ideal time to complete unfinished projects around the house. Whenever my mother brought up similar topics, my father's standard reply was, "You're right. We'll have to sit down one of these days and discuss it. But you know the timing has to be *just right*."

Of course, the right time never came. Some other priority or need took precedence, but on this particular occasion, Mother decided that things would be different. Her look of determination left little doubt in my mind that would come out on top.

"Dear," she said to my father, "I think we need to contemplate getting away for a weekend and enjoying ourselves."

Barely listening, my father eagerly thumbed through the newspaper in search of the sports section. His reply to her was half-hearted, "Good idea," he said despondently, "let's keep that in mind when the *timing is right*. You know, the kids have school, but next summer . . ."

Mother interrupted him politely, "You're right, of course, but I have wonderful news," she declared. "The children have a long weekend coming up, and this would be the ideal time to visit Niagara Falls. What do you think?"

Father folded the newspaper and placed it on his lap. "The kids may be off, but you always work that weekend taking inventory," he pointed out, with a bit of a smirk crossing his face. Confidently, he returned to the newspaper, but not for long.

"Good news, dear," replied my mother. "This is the first time in years that I have that weekend off. It's Labor Day."

The pressure beginning to mount, he laid his paper aside and moved up against the table, assuming his defensive, hard negotiating mode. "That's all well and good," he said, "but given the fact that it's a holiday weekend, there's no way we'll be able to get a reservation. You have to book those types of weekends well in advance."

Undeterred, Mother had a solution. "I *can't* seem to run out of good news!" she declared. "I anticipated that possibility, so I booked the room a few months ago—just in case it might work out."

Beads of perspiration began forming on his forehead, and his lips started twitching, revealing his desperate nature. "Fine," he argued, becoming unreasonably enraged, "but haven't you forgotten the dog? He HATES KENNELS!"

Father's composure dissolved as he ranted, "Remember the last time we went away? He didn't eat for three days!"

Mother's deadpan look gave Father a false sense of security, so she rebounded, saying, "You're not going to believe this, but our neighbor *loves* the dog— and he loves her; so, when I told her our plans, she volunteered to watch him. A real stroke of luck, huh?" His eyes narrowed and his body stiffened. It was time to play hardball.

"Do you remember the last time we tried to reach a consensus? It never worked!" he pointed out, but once again, the wizard pulled another rabbit out of her hat.

"No problem," said Mother, calmly. "Niagara Falls has it all! Indoor tennis for Charles; hiking trails for Robert; museums and fine restaurants for me; and there's even a 24/7 championship bowling lane for the head of the household. Did I mention the fact that it's within walking distance of the hotel?"

Father was up against the ropes, and he knew it. Now there were only two issues remaining, but they were big ones: *price* and *ego*.

"It all sounds great," he said, "but who's going to pay for this wonderful weekend?"

Mother appeared uncertain, and father's eyes sparkled, but not for long. "I knew this would be a major concern, so I booked it well in advance. And here's the *really* good news," she said, struggling to hide a smug look. "They gave us a forty percent discount, which includes breakfast *and* lunch! Is that great or what?"

Wearing a pained expression, Father made a last-ditch effort. "So who's going to do all the driving?" Mother graciously volunteered to share that responsibility.

Victorious, she looked him in the eye and softly said, "I want this time away for *all* us, not just me and the boys. You deserve a break just as much as anyone."

Then she looked at us and said, "Boys, it's time to do your homework. I've already done mine." My father reached into his pocket, pulled out a white handkerchief and waved it. My brother and I began singing, "O'Canada," which made my father laugh and finally get with the program as he chimed in.

The next day, I couldn't resist asking Mother about her methods of persuasion. "What's your secret?" I inquired.

"When you call it a *secret*, this suggests that I'm trying to talk someone into something, but this couldn't be further from the truth," she explained, looking at me with concern. "I think the key to persuading people is to let them make up their own minds. People don't resist change; they resist being told or threatened to change. For example, the three of us wanted to go to Canada, but your father didn't; so I had to satisfy all of his objections, and I did."

"That's fine, but deep down inside, I don't think he honestly wanted to go," I pointed out.

"That's true," she conceded, adding, "and I knew it. I had to give him a good reason he could accept. I had to help him share our desire to go, because the truth is; he needs and deserves this weekend of relaxation as much as we do. You see, Robert, if people believe that you have their best interests at heart, you have an excellent chance of them going along with you."

It suddenly occurred to me that she had just handed me the *key* to unlocking her secret. "Okay, it all makes sense now," I told her, smugly adding, "Are you happy that I finally agree?"

Without missing a beat, she replied, "It's not important that *I'm* happy, what's most important is that *you* are."

The *sage of sages* had done it once again! She didn't convince me of anything; I ultimately convinced myself, and that was the secret of her success. Over the years, I had countless opportunities to apply her theory, and more often than not, I was successful. There was one particular experience, however, that stands out in my mind.

It was Christmastime in New York, and I had just left a client's office to do some shopping during lunch. It was a cold and blustery day; but I wasn't wearing a coat, as usual. I find them cumbersome and uncomfortable. Better to get pneumonia than be practical, right? After dodging taxis and pedestrians, I entered the holiday Mecca of tradition, style, prestige and warmth: Bloomingdales! Decked out in Christmas colors and sparkled from top to bottom, Bloomie's was bustling with holiday shoppers from all over the world.

Some find the holiday mayhem disconcerting; but I find it invigorating. I deftly weaved my way through the shopping bag-laden crowd on my way to the men's department. When I arrived in front of the suit department,

I stood motionless for a moment, just savoring the spirit of the captains of industry, fashion, theater, and literature who had shopped here before me. My reverie was short-lived when I heard a voice behind me say, "Excuse me, but do you work here?" I looked around before realizing that a strikingly handsome young man was speaking to me.

I'm guessing that my lack of a coat may have given him the impression that I was a sales clerk, but when I thought about it, I realized that this has been a pattern in my life. No matter the time of year, I'm inevitably approached and asked the same question: "Do you work here?"

I was on the verge of saying no, when I suddenly gave into my holiday-induced whimsical side, and decided to go along with his assumption. "Yes," I answered, smiling broadly. "How may I help you?"

I visualized myself standing in this man's shoes some 20 years earlier. I thought, if I can help this young man, what harm could come of it? I figured that if nothing else, the time I spent with him could be a great learning experience for both of us. Out of the corner of my eye, I spotted an actual sales clerk observing my actions; he looked concerned.

"I'm looking for a suit," the young man told me. I guessed that he might be a recent college graduate entering the world of business for the first time, in need of proper business attire. His stance was a mix between confidence and self-doubt.

I asked him, "Why do you need a suit?

His answer confirmed my guess. "I just graduated from MIT's School of Engineering, and I've accepted a position with Gulf Oil," he told me rather excitedly. "I'm going to be a supervisor on an offshore drilling rig, and at the start of each month, I have to make a presentation to senior management on the quality and grade of the oil production at our headquarters in Baton Rouge, Louisiana."

This was his first job, his first suit, and perhaps he might consider opening his first department store charge account. The first step was to select a suit that fit his needs. "I want something attractive and versatile," he told me. "I want a suit that I can wear for different formal occasions, not just work."

He told me his size—a perfect 42 long. He was in luck, because Bloomie's is well known for selling one of the best off-the-rack custom suits, you can buy—Hickey Freeman—and they were on sale. With a retail price tag of approximately $800, they had been marked down for a limited time to $375. His size was well represented.

As we headed over to a rack of Hickey Freeman's, I suggested that he first open a charge account, because I knew that new accounts receive an additional 15 percent off their first purchase. He jumped at the chance, so I asked one of the real sales associates for an application. Without challenging my authority, the sales clerk retrieved an application and handed it to the customer. I wondered why the sales clerk didn't' question my identity. Then I assumed he thought I was someone in management, just passing through. *First test passed,* I thought to myself.

The next step was selecting the perfect all-occasion suit. Given his short-and long-term personal and business goals, I told him that I thought it would be in his best interest to consider buying *two* classic pinstripes: one in navy blue and the other in brown. "Buying both of these will give you greater versatility and longer wear," I explained, and he agreed. *Second test passed!* I mentally gave myself a high-five.

I told him about the benefits he would gain, versus his investment. "For $750, you're getting two suits for the price of one, plus an additional 15 percent discount," I pointed out, noting the fact that he could even pay off the suits in monthly installments, since we would now have a charge card.

He agreed that he could comfortably meet the monthly payments. Clearly thrilled about his purchase, he heartily shook my hand. "Thank you so much, Robert!" he said with sincerity. "Bloomingdale's is lucky to have professionals like you representing them." I inwardly cringed with guilt, but accepted the compliment. *Third test passed,* I thought to myself. *Game, set, and match!*

At that point, I turned the sale over to my loyal sales associate/observer. After the young man had left (with a spring in his step, mind you), the sales clerk thanked me for the commission. "Not to be ungrateful," he said, "But who are you?"

I told him that I was a visiting buyer; just passing through. "I'm not really a sales associate," I confided, and he seemed satisfied by my explanation. Why not? After all, this was New York City!

As I left the store, I reflected on the experience. My first thought was about how much I had enjoyed the whole affair. My second thought was about how my mother would have assessed my behavior. I'm certain she wouldn't have been pleased with me misrepresenting myself, but at the same time, I think she would have found the outcome acceptable. She always emphasized that our *intent* is the barometer for our actions.

If the motives are to bring a positive outcome to all interested parties, then the action should be given the benefit of the doubt. In this case, the customer got exactly what he wanted . . . and more! In fact, his purchase on that day provided that young man a leg up on beginning his career on a positive note. The sales clerk was equally satisfied, because he received on-the-job training and a nice commission. For me, it was an opportunity to set Mother's principles into practice once again . . . while having a little fun in the process. Admittedly, I did pay a price that day: I forgot to do my own shopping!

DIGNITY

Mother always said, "Robert . . .
most people can survive the loss of most things in life, but the loss of self-respect and dignity is too great a price for anyone to pay."

IN MY YOUTH, I SPENT a great deal of time helping out in my mother's shoe store. My primary duties included taking inventory, dusting shoeboxes, sweeping floors, etc. While I was working, I was also observing my mother's masterful sales techniques.

To this day, I marvel at the way she could wait on numerous customers at the same time and still make each one of them feel as though they were her only customer. She once told me that she attributed her success to the fact that she satisfied customer's specific needs, all the while building a strong, personal relationship with them.

In my own observations, I noticed that all of her sales began with friendly banter about the health and latest developments in her customers' lives. The purchasing of shoes appeared to be more of an afterthought. It didn't matter if you were a doctor, lawyer, steel mill worker, or homemaker . . . you received exactly the same level of professionalism and respect.

Mrs. Goldberg was a lifelong friend and customer. One day, she spied the new spring line in the window and entered the store, determined to buy one in every color. Unfortunately, the new styles only came in narrow and medium widths, but her size ranged closer to the snowshoe category. It was obvious the shoes wouldn't fit; however, Mrs. Goldberg's initial desire turned into a magnificent obsession.

Acutely aware of that fact, Mother went back into the stockroom and returned with the widest width she had in stock. Like a child on Christmas morning, Mrs. Goldberg's eyes glittered with anticipation. Eagerly, she tried the shoe on, but to no avail. She struggled and pulled, wiggled and turned, and failed once again. In a move reminiscent of Cinderella's stepsisters, she tried to cram her foot into the shoe as beads of perspiration broke out on her forehead in frustration. Well aware of Mrs. Goldberg's history of high blood pressure, Mother became concerned.

"Molly, would you like to look at some other styles?" Mother gently asked, but Mrs. Goldberg didn't reply. She eventually crammed her feet into the too-small shoes, if *on* is defined by all of her toes being hidden and two-thirds of her heels sticking out!

She looked worn out, but she still seemed pleased with her progress . . . until my mother said, "How do they feel, Molly?"

Mrs. Goldberg answered breathlessly, as though stuck between two Sumo wrestlers. "They're great!" she gasped. "They're just a l-i-t-t-l-e tight in the heel."

Without judgment, Mother said, "Good. Please stand up, so I can check them." A concerned look on her face, Mrs. Goldberg slowly began to rise. When she was upright, her expression turned to that of momentary victory; and then the painful reality set in. It was quite clear, from the grimace she was making, that her feet were in agony, but still she persevered. After all, she made a significant investment and expected a fair return.

Freudian theory states that each of us has an ego. Then there are those who have an *Eggo*—a double dose. Our Mrs. Goldberg was 4-G's and rising. She wasn't just a fashion plate; she was a service for 12! In an effort to shift the responsibility, she asked my mother, "Dorothy, what do you think?"

Trying not to be obvious about the fact that I was closely observing their interaction, I pretended to sweep the floor close by as I anxiously awaited another lesson from the Master of Diplomacy—I wasn't disappointed.

My mother paused, studied the shoes and offered her final verdict: "Well, Molly, you *know* I've never liked you in pastels!"

Mrs. Goldberg breathed a sigh of relief. "You're right, "she said to my mother as she quickly pried her feet out of the shoes. "Neither do I." In dismissing the offending shoes, Mrs. Goldberg's ego remained intact, and a much better fit was in the wings.

Later that evening, I discussed the Mrs. Goldberg incident with my mother. "Mother," I pointed out, "you weren't totally honest with her, were you?"

"I can see where you might have that opinion," she replied. "But there were other things that needed to be taken into consideration. First, if I convinced her to buy those shoes, it would only be a matter of time before they were returned, if she kept them because she didn't want to offend me, she would have wasted her money. In either case, her level of trust in my ability as a professional saleswoman would have suffered."

Mother reminded me that it takes a lifetime to build respect, but only a second to lose it. "That may not seem fair," she added, "but life is not often fair, and there's no guarantee that it ever will be." I hated hearing that, but I knew she was right.

Then she told me about the importance of preserving one's dignity. "Dignity," she said, "is the same thing as self-respect and the respect for others. You see, when someone has their heart set on something, it is sometimes difficult for them to let go without some degree of satisfaction or justification. Always make sure that your dignity—and that of others—be taken into account." As always, Mother passed with flying colors—*pastel colors*—that is.

Many years later, I was living in West Berlin. One day, I was watching an extraordinary street juggler practicing his craft . . . with more than just his skill hanging in the balance.

Berlin is a haven for amateur entertainers, and during the height of the tourist season, I always enjoyed watching the many performers as they showed off their talents on the city's street corners. I was watching this juggler extraordinaire; thinking that not only did he exhibit unerring dexterity, I was also impressed with the way he accompanied his craft with a spontaneous monologue of one-liners that had the crowd mesmerized.

At the end of his performance, he received a thunderous ovation. As is customary, he passed his hat, but many in the front row balked at his request. Those in the second row, where I was standing, were never even given a chance to contribute.

Initially, he seemed to brush it off, but as I watched, the pattern continued without explanation. His eyes filled with disbelief and justifiable resentment. He slowly lowered his hat and turned away from the audience.

Silently, he gathered his paraphernalia and prepared to depart. Some members of the audience—driven more by guilt than generosity—attempted to interrupt with an offering. In German, he politely but firmly said, "No, thank you. You keep it. I don't want charity; I just wanted your respect and appreciation, but I apparently got neither."

Repeatedly, others tried to hand him money, but he was so deeply hurt and shaken that he could not even look them in the eye. I waited until most of the audience had dispersed before attempting to approach him.

When he regained his composure and began preparing for his next performance, I sidled up to him and quietly inquired in German, "Has this ever happened to you before?"

He looked at me wide-eyed before he shook his head and whispered, "Nie mals." *Never.*

"Sometimes, it's difficult to understand why people act as they do," I offered, switching over to English.

"Ja," was his reply, and he looked at me inquisitively. At that point, for what it was worth, I felt compelled to offer my opinion. I said, "Well, I think that you are not only skilled, but you're also extraordinarily gifted. The monologue and impromptu comments were exceptional."

He smiled modestly, and replied in English, "Thank you."

He started to turn away from me, but I just had to know why he had so adamantly refused the offers that the audience subsequently made.

I questioned him, and he repeated what he had said before about how they were apparently just giving out of guilt and pity—not out of sincere appreciation for his work.

"I am insulted," he shrugged.

"I understand," I told him as I pulled some bills out of my wallet and handed them to him. He held up his hand in resistance, but I insisted. "*This* donation is in acknowledgment and respect of your efforts and obvious talent. No other reason."

He eventually accepted the money, and said graciously, "Vielen dank." *Many thanks.* Even though no one can predict how future audiences would react to him, I was certain that the juggler would always respond with the same quiet dignity.

REALITY

Mother always said, "Robert . . .
deal with what is, and not
what you think it should be."

WHENEVER THINGS DIDN'T GO MY WAY, I would ask my mother, *why?*

"Why, Mom? Why does it have to be that way?"

She always had the same, exasperated reply; "Because that's just the way it is!" she would say through clenched teeth. "I've explained the reasons to you, but you're not willing to accept them. Now, please don't ask me again!"

My incessant whining was a hot-button topic, but I never wanted to admit it. I assumed, by asking the same question over and over again, the situation might change, and I would eventually get want I wanted; sadly, it never worked out that way, it just made matters worse. My annoying behavior was the result of my not wanting to accept the reality of a particular situation.

"Robert, if you deal with what *is,* and not what you think *should* be; you will not only eliminate the problem much more quickly, in the end, you will be happier and more productive."

During my school years, not following this advice had negative implications for me. For example, upon being advised that a term paper in history was due two weeks earlier than originally scheduled, my first reaction was, *this isn't fair! How could he do this to me?* Although I knew the date wouldn't change, it took me at least two days to overcome my frustration with the unfairness of it all before I started to work toward meeting the shorter deadline.

Not only did I waste two days, but I was so focused on negative thoughts, that once I finally accepted the reality of the new due date, it took me yet *another* two days to gain a positive attitude and enough momentum to complete the project on time.

Mother would watch me go through this destructive cycle, but she remained silent on the subject . . . that, is, unless I goaded her on. *Then* she gave me her pat answer and tried to extricate herself from my presence. Of course, she knew then that my mind was in its least-receptive state. So, she just let me go through it again and again and again—experiencing anger and self-pity before reaching eventual acceptance of the reality of any given situation.

I finally completed the paper, but only one day before it was due. My mother sensed it was time for one of our *little chats*, which meant, counseling time—which was always fine with me, because they were, indeed, little. Most often, short and to the point, whatever she was about to tell me would doubtlessly be meaningful.

"How do you feel about completing that history paper on time?" was her lead question.

"I'm just glad it's over!" I exclaimed.

"I'll bet!" she replied before asking, "But what did you learn from this experience?"

"Never to trust teachers!" I said with a smirk on my face, knowing that this was not the answer she wanted to hear.

She glared right back, and countered with, "You don't really mean that—do you?"

"No . . ." I sheepishly admitted, "I just felt like it was so *unfair*!"

"Many things in life are unfair," she gently reminded me before launching off on her usual advice. "If something you don't like can't be changed, then the only option is to deal with it, whether you like it or not. The sooner you attack the problem, the sooner it goes away."

"I guess you're right," I reluctantly admitted for the umpteenth time.

She remained undeterred and pressed on. "What *else* did you learn?"

My answer surprised her. "Not to waste time pouting over something that's not going to change, no matter how hard I try to wish it away. As you always say, Mother, deal with what *is* and not what you think should be, right?" A sudden smile brightened her previously dark expression, and she knew at that point it I finally understood her point.

In jest, she said, while tapping me on the head, "There's still hope for you!"

Many years later, while working in Stuttgart, West Germany, I was asked to speak at a workshop conference for the manager of an American engineering company that was experiencing an unexpected downturn. Business had suddenly dropped off by 25 percent, so management hired me to help solve their problems.

When I questioned the managers about what they were doing to deal with the situation, they said that all employees had been advised to cut back immediately on expenditures; which meant no travel, in addition to counting staples and rubber bands.

Then I asked, "What formal announcements have been made to let your employees know about the severity of this situation?

Not wanting to alarm anyone unnecessarily, one of the managers admitted that they had kept quiet about what was going on. "We figured that this would all pass in time, and things would eventually return to normal," he rationalized.

"It's generally known that frontline personnel are usually the first to know exactly what the state of business is," I pointed out, adding, "Using subterfuge to avoid panic could easily create a deeper problem than what you are already experiencing because of the economic situation."

"Worse?" They all looked alarmed. "What could be worse?"

"Your employees will lose respect for you," I answered, looking each one of them straight in the eye. "The anxiety you tried to avoid *will* happen, and your productivity—and ultimately your profits—will get *worse*."

I softened that blow by telling them that by dealing with the situation in an honest, open and direct manner, they could take advantage of it.

"How?" Their expressions brightened.

It was nearing lunchtime, so I thought that this would be a good time to take a break. I also needed some time to collect my thoughts and formulate some ideas. "Let's break for lunch, and then I'll present my plan," I said, although what I was really thinking was, *Robert, this had better be good.* In asking *them* to look at reality, I found myself having to do the same.

While I prepared my notes during lunch, one of the company officers walked up to me and said, smiling wryly, "You've piqued our curiosity; now we expect you to satisfy it."

When we reconvened, the air of expectation in the room was thick. I began with, "Mother always said, 'Robert, deal with what is, not what you think *should* be.'"

Using that oft-heard phrase bolstered me to continue. I explained, "Business will have its difficult times, and how you handle those downturns will set the tone when business begins to improve. In fact, it can be a catalyst for making the turnaround occur even sooner than expected; and serve as a momentum builder as well." The managers looked incredibly engaged and even hopeful as I spoke. Smiling, I added, "It's the *attitude* you bring to the situation that will determine the actions you take in a tough market."

I then proposed the following, "What if your employees were to hear an announcement like this: 'Ladies and gentlemen, we are experiencing a *temporary* drop in business. None of us knows how long this situation will persist, but that's not what's important right now. What we need to do is take advantage of this situation, because it gives us an excellent opportunity to do some things we don't usually have time to do when business is good."

I listed a few of the ways they could make the most out of the lag in production. I suggested conducting an in-depth analysis to determine how well they are serving their existing customer base, along with ways in which they could serve them better. In addition, define new business development strategies; review and assess their existing marketing plan and make any necessary adjustments; along with updating internal operating procedures, policies and systems; and review and improve working relationships between departments.

I explained that while it wasn't the specific content wasn't the issue, as much as the intent and potential effect this announcement would have on their employees. "It's during times like these when a company has an opportunity to show its true character and capability for leadership," adding, "the announcement also serves as a model of behavior for every individual and department when addressing their daily challenges."

"As Mother often said, 'it is *how* you react under pressure that people will long remember.'" I further noted that honesty and grace under pressure, from management, sets the stage for improving long-term motivation and loyalty from its employees.

It was gratifying to see the level of enthusiasm from all of the managers given their full support behind the recommendation. To be clear, it wasn't a vote of confidence for Mother or me; it was an affirmation that management finally recognized that dealing with reality in the most direct and positive manner is a more effective and efficient way of conducting business—no matter how challenging or difficult the circumstances. As Mother always said, *"Robert, deal with what is, not what you think or wish it could or should be." Take* what you are given and make the *most* of it; and quite often, you might surprise yourself on how successful you can be.

COMMUNICATION

Mother always said, "Robert . . .
communicating is a lot like farming
—you have to till the soil before you plant the seeds."

MOTHER'S RURAL UPBRINGING PREDISPOSED HER to use farming-related sayings to illustrate her lessons. One of her favorites was, "If you don't till the soil before you plant the seeds, they just wash away, and then you've wasted your time." She believed that the same principle applied when communicating with people: if you properly till the mental soil of your listener before planting your thoughts or ideas, the quality of the exchange will dramatically improve. She also said it gave people fewer places to hide. This was especially true when the topic centered on school and my grades.

At the end of each grading period, I always expected Mother to approach me for one of our talks. Before she would begin, however, she would make sure that I had a chance to give her an idea of how I thought my grades had turned out. One year, my assessment was this: "I think I did pretty well: 3 A's, 3 B's, and 3 C's."

"On average, that's not bad," she replied before bringing up the damning details. "What were the subjects? Show me your report card." Reluctantly, I pulled it out of my backpack.

She announced the grades as she read them; "An 'A' in English . . . an 'A' in citizenship . . ." and then she added, "I certainly wouldn't expect anything less." At least I hadn't come up short.

She continued, " . . . an 'A' in gym . . ."

Then she ran out of A's. "A 'B' in geography . . . a 'B' in art . . . a 'B' in music . . ." at this point, I watched her expression as it went from her *that's not bad* look before deteriorating into her devastated *I've-just-run-out of A's and B's* look. "A 'C' in Math?" she said, rhetorically—at least I hoped so. Her smile became a memory as she continued listing my next two disappointments: A 'C' in science and a 'C' in handwriting.

With the preliminaries out of the way, the battle began. "Are you pleased with these grades?" she asked me; her expression was that of a woman who was obviously *not* pleased.

"I'm pleased if you're pleased," I quipped, nervously trying to bring the tension down. "Are you pleased?"

She parried with a deadpan, "What do you think?"

"I don't know . . . ," I answered, looking down at my shoes.

I survived that particular skirmish with an admonition that the distribution of grades had to be realigned. She offered some helpful hints, concluded with a summary of what she wanted me to do and checked my understanding by making me repeat her instructions in my own words. After numerous clarifications, the talk finally ended.

Even though these encounters weren't always pleasant, I considered them less threatening and more productive than I would have, had she handled them differently. In fact, I went through so many of these sessions that the process couldn't help but become a permanent fixture in my mind. As a result, they eventually served me well in my business career—especially during annual reviews of my performance.

Annual reviews—no one likes them, not the evaluator or the one being evaluated. Even with some of today's sophisticated evaluation systems, human unpredictability is still a critical factor. For just this reason, evaluators try to get through the process in as little time as possible, with as little conflict as necessary.

My manager was no exception to the rule. His modus operandi was to schedule reviews for the last ten minutes of the day, just prior to leaving for the airport for a trip to some faraway destination. On one occasion, I was looking forward to my review, because I had one of my best years ever; in fact, I was so eager, I momentarily forgot about his typical strategy.

He scheduled my review for a Friday at 5 p.m. sharp. When I arrived, he told me what I should have already known that he had to catch a 6:30 flight to Asia that evening, so my time with him would be limited to thirty minutes, not the standard, ninety or more.

"Look, Robert," he said, shuffling his papers and obviously distracted with the task of leaving for another continent. "I don't have much time, but I wanted you to know that I think you're a nice, hardworking guy, and you did a darn good job for us this year."

While speaking, he handed me a piece of ripped-out notebook paper that had a percentage raise written on it with a number so low, I could qualify for government welfare. Looking totally preoccupied, he emphasized the need to expedite the discussion. What he didn't know was that I had prepared a strategy in the event this situation would occur—and was I glad that I did.

Thinking of my mother, I decided to pick a plow start tilling! I started off by letting him know that I was sympathetic to the fact that he was busy. I said, "Mr. Jones, I recognize your time constraints, but I was wondering if I could take just 20 minutes of your time to share my thoughts on my evaluation . . . from *both* of our perspectives."

He didn't immediately shut me down, so before he could say anything else, I quickly continued my train of thought, adding, "I thought we might take a quick look at specific requirements and then assess how I did in a way that will further my understanding of your expectations and perceptions of my work. I was also hoping that you might share with me ways in which I can improve, so that I will be better equipped to keep meeting your and the company's goals. All I ask for is 20 minutes of your time; I promise I won't let you miss your flight."

He sat back in his chair and let out a deep sigh before replying, "Ahh . . . sure, go ahead, but you better be quick."

After thanking him, I listed the specific goals in my job description, along with the numbers my department had achieved. One by one, we covered what was expected and the scheduled percentage increases for achieving each goal. We also covered the areas in which I needed to develop, and by focusing on specific issues, we avoided personal conflicts. In fact, I was surprised to find that his perceptions were very insightful; and it all happened within the allotted amount of time.

Mother always emphasized to me that the beginning of a conversation is usually the most important part of any discussion. She would say, "Robert, be as objective as possible; always take into consideration the needs of all interested parties."

Thanks to my handling of the situation, my raise went from a fraction to a whole number, and my boss appeared to be pleased with the way this particular review turned out. One thing I am certain; he made his plane. I know this, because I drove him to the airport.

OPINIONS

Mother always said, "Robert . . .
remember—there are three sides to every story, two opinions and the truth falls somewhere in between."

EVERY TIME I OFFERED MY opinion or judgment about someone or something of relative importance, Mother would ask, "Why do you feel that way? What facts did you base your opinion on?"

Defensively I would reply, "Can't I have a personal opinion?"

She would matter-of-factly explain that she was just curious as to how I had arrived at my opinion. Nevertheless, I knew what she was really getting at; she had sensed a less-than-objective attitude on my part, and her radar was always accurate. Her approach was effective, and always delivered in a constructive manner. As a result of her needling, I eventually found myself taking on more responsibility for what I was saying and why.

While working in her store, I often had the opportunity to observe my mother practice what she preached, but there was one time that stands out in my mind. It was a typical Saturday in western Pennsylvania, when a well-dressed, professional-looking man entered the shoe store. Mother greeted him and asked if she could be of assistance. It turns out that he was attending a local fund-raiser that evening and needed a pair of dress shoes, so Mother showed him several suitable models.

He was not a regular customer, so she asked if he was from out of town. "I'm originally from New England, but presently working and living in New York City," he explained, before asking her, "Have you ever been to New York?"

"Yes," she replied. "I loved it! It's so big and exciting and full of energy." Suddenly, a scowl clouded his expression. "You must be kidding me!" he practically spat. "It's the *worst* city in the world!"

Watching this exchange, I thought, *uh-oh—forget this sale*! Then I considered whom he was dealing with and decided not to count Mother out just yet . . .

Mother exhibited no outward signs of defensiveness. She paused then offered a disarming smile, and then in a gentle, non-judgmental tone, replied, "I'd be very interested in knowing why you feel the way you do."

Looking more composed, he told her about the dangers of the big city. "The crowds are enormous, and the traffic and noise can drive you crazy; there's crime and filth, and it costs a fortune to buy *anything*!"

"You're right," she acknowledged. "Those can be difficult and frustrating things to deal with."

The unexpected response left him guarded, so he checked for understanding by asking, "Are you saying you agree with me?"

"Yes . . . and no," she replied, adding, "I think it comes down to one's own point of view. I mean, everything you say is true to a degree, but I would think that most major cities have those types of problems." Looking intrigued, he nodded his head in agreement, so she continued, "That being the case, my approach has always been that there are positives and negatives in *everything*. Knowing that, I personally try and make the best of every situation I find myself in. For example, what—if anything—do *you* find interesting, unique and enjoyable in the city?"

He bit his lip, his brow furrowed in thought before he replied, "Well, the theaters and entertainment are hard to beat."

"Anything else?" she prompted.

"The restaurants are some of the best in the world, and the shopping is unlimited," he pointed out before a slow smile crossed his face—the previously dirty city had taken on a bit of a sparkle. The debate continued for a while longer before he said, "I guess this confirms the adage, 'There are two sides to every story.'"

Mother's reply took him off guard. "Oh? I was always taught that there are *three*."

"Three?"

My mother nodded. "Of course," she said, "two opinions and the truth."

As the words registered, he began laughing. "You know what?" he said to her, "you're absolutely right! I never thought of it that way." On that day,

Mother made *two* sales: one was a pair of men's dress shoes, and the other was a pair of opinions that began moving closer to the truth.

Opinions and judgments come in many degrees of intensity and appear in a variety of situations. One of the most pleasant experiences I ever had occurred when maturity and credibility ran head-on into youth and inexperience. The battle lines were drawn, but the outcome resulted in both parties sharing the spoils with an unlikely hero.

I attended a conference in Stuttgart, West Germany, held by the US Army Corps of Engineers for local private contractors. The conference was designed to improve relations between the various parties and enhance their productivity. Over the years, I had done a substantial amount of consulting for the Corps and would frequently attend workshops to increase my knowledge and establish local contacts. At this particular conference, the speakers were well known and respected by the audience, except for one young engineer. A specialist in contracts, she had an excellent reputation within the Corps, but she had not yet proven herself with the private contractors.

She had just made her introductory comments when a seasoned-looking gentleman with a sour expression on his face raised his hand and said, "Young lady, with no personal disrespect to you, I believe this topic requires someone who has a greater degree of experience. May I suggest a more senior member of your organization handle this portion of the presentation?" She looked shocked.

In the next moment, she regained her composure and replied, "Sir, if I understand correctly, it's your opinion that my qualifications and experience are inadequate. Is that right?"

He looked a bit startled, and then nodded his head affirmatively.

She continued, "Given my limited direct work experience with contractors, I understand why you may have drawn that conclusion. However, I have prepared what I think will be an interesting, informative, and practical presentation. My overall objective is to review proposed changes in contract policies and procedures to increase productivity and avoid costly misinterpretations for both parties. I encourage you and the other members of the conference to offer your experienced opinions to determine the value of what I suggest."

For the next hour, she led a lively discussion of existing policies and proposed changes. She gave each side a fair opportunity to state their opinion until a consensus was reached, and when most of the presentation's objectives had been met; she announced a short coffee break.

When we returned to complete the session, many of the participants made it a point to commend her on her efforts. Afterwards, I noticed that her original antagonist waited until most of the audience had left before walking up to her.

"Young lady, I misjudged you," he told her. "I assumed that your age and experience were insufficient, but I was wrong."

"Your concern over my inexperience was valid," she graciously replied. "I'm just pleased that I was able to bring sufficient value to the discussion."

As he walked away, I approached her and introduced myself. "Congratulations on an excellent presentation," I said.

Her reply was swift. "Well, as Mother always said, there are three sides to every story; two opinions and the truth."

Shocked, I said, "Excuse me, but where did you hear that?"

Her smile was genuine as she explained, "You don't remember me, but I attended one of your workshops several years ago, when you told the story of the New Yorker and your mother." "Well, that's certainly one on me," I said, and we both had a good laugh.

Mother often said, "Although opinions are frequently considered personal in nature, they can, however, serve to increase our credibility and degree of influence on others, if they are based upon sound logic and facts." *Of course, that is only her opinion.*

HUMILIATION

Mother always said, "Robert . . .
humiliation is the worst form of embarrassment a person can experience."

MOTHER'S TEACHINGS COVERED MANY BEHAVIORS that she found almost unforgivable, but none was as heartbreaking to her as one human being humiliating another. Infringing on every personal and religious belief she had, Mother considered humiliation to be one of the most degrading forms of embarrassment anyone could experience or witness.

She would say, "Once you've been humiliated, you may be able to forgive, but it's unlikely you'll ever forget."

"Why is humiliation so terrible?" I once asked her.

"Because it takes away a part of your soul," she replied, "and that isn't easily repaired." At the tender age of eleven, it was a concept beyond my years, but it didn't take long before I understood.

Mother often observed that children could be crueler out of ignorance than adults by intent could. That was a difficult concept for me to grasp, until I witnessed it. Mother always taught me that the true worth of a person isn't based on how much money he has, but what he is like as a person. To think or behave otherwise is contrary to what is truly valuable in life; unfortunately, not everyone feels that way.

For example, take the bus I rode to school each day: We didn't have assigned seating, but most of the children occupied the same seats every day. Everyone sat with a friend, but there was one girl who always sat alone. She sat directly behind the driver, and I never even noticed her until one day, so I asked one of my friends who she was.

He looked at me incredulously. "You don't know? She is a girl from down the road who wears the same dress every day. Everyone says her family doesn't even have a bathroom in their house! No one would be caught dead talking to her!"

As the year progressed, the other children relentlessly harassed this girl. They made fun of her unusually deep voice and the fact that she wore the same dress almost daily.

One day, the harassment hit a fever pitch when a group of children formed a circle around her on the playground and began yelling, "We don't like poor girls! Why don't you go live somewhere else?"

She stood motionless amongst them, absorbing their verbal blows in silence for the longest time, until she finally lost her composure and fell to the ground, weeping piteously. One of the teachers finally intervened, and as the children scattered, she helped the girl to her feet and tenderly walked her into the office.

Witnessing this incident, I suddenly knew what Mother had meant. Watching the girl being taunted and bullied caused me intense pain and embarrassment. I couldn't imagine anyone being treated so cruelly! I didn't think that she would return to school the next day, but she did.

I witnessed the same cruelty many years later in West Berlin, which is quite an unlikely backdrop for such an incident, because of the city's desire to erase its historic legacy of violence.

I was living in Berlin at the time, and I was looking forward to the coming of summer—the season of outdoor cafes, seemingly endless hours of sunlight, stimulating conversation and an indescribable serenity that fills the heart and mind. During summers, the streets of Berlin become a sea of humanity, featuring representatives from every corner of the earth and all speaking different languages, but still united by humanity.

Prior to the dismantling of the infamous Berlin Wall, the city stood as a political island, isolated only by its geography. Living in this "bubble" created a bond that was proudly acknowledged by all who dwelled within the alluring German city.

Once the Berlin Wall was torn down, the city adapted to its new reality, but its heart and soul will always remain uniquely *Berlin.*

Come springtime, large crowds form on every street corner to watch jugglers, mimes and musicians practice their skills. Many of these performers are university students, using their talents as a means to supplementing their income.

One day, I was seated at a sidewalk cafe on the edge of the famous intersection of Kurfurstendamm and Joachimsthalerstrasse. The Cafe Kranzler was packed with a supportive audience enjoying the antics of one of Berlin's finest mimes. As part of his act, the mime would intentionally walk toward an approaching passerby; then, when the victim passed him, the mime would turn and follow directly behind. The mime's uncanny ability to mimic the unwary stranger's gait and mannerisms made the performance hilarious. It was a superb show.

Repeatedly, a new pedestrian became an unwitting victim, until a rather tall, slender man, approximately 30 years of age, shamefully broke the pattern. Everything was going as planned, until the man unexpectedly turned and spat directly into the mime's face. In front of the shocked audience, the man began throwing wild punches, striking the mime a number of times, all the while screaming obscenities in German. I, along with several hundred spectators, stood gape-mouthed as we watched the mine fend off his attacker with the palms of his hand outstretched before standing frozen on the street corner, stunned. A veil of silence fell over the crowd, and the happiness of the day seemed suddenly and hopelessly lost.

His head lowered, the mime softly apologized to the attacker and then turned away while the crowd began verbally admonishing the man's behavior. When they started threatening to call the police, the angry man rushed off. The crowd fell silent again, and it struck me that this was undoubtedly one of the more humiliating experiences any human being can suffer.

His back to the crowd, neither the mime nor his audience uttered a word. We all just stood there, waiting for his reaction. After a bit, the mime turned and raised his hands as if to gesture to the audience that he needed more time to pull himself together. Then, we watched him walk back to his staging area, pretend to wipe off his face, and replaced it with a new one. Once he completed this procedure, he stood motionless, his eyes staring down at the ground.

The moment before his resumed his performance turned into an eternity. He could have packed up and left, and no one would have faulted him, but he didn't. He instead flashed the crowd a dazzling smile, and then continued on as though nothing had happened. When he started following behind another hapless victim, the spontaneous roar from the onlookers was deafening.

After completing his performance, the mime offered his hat for the traditional contributions. I noticed that he was being generously rewarded for both his unique talent and the courage he'd exhibited. Admiration and respect filled the eyes of everyone he passed, and words of encouragement and appreciation rained down upon him as he greeted his fans.

Watching this display, I thought to myself that this was more than just an outstanding demonstration of courage and professionalism. What began as an unpleasant incident ended up creating an unexpected bond between the mime and his audience. What would usually have been only a superficial relationship was now a special, personal one. In this one, random incident, I saw a glimmer of hope for the preservation of basic human decency.

RESPECT

Father always said, "Robert . . .
it takes a lifetime to build respect
—and only a second to lose it
—it doesn't seem quite fair,
but no one promised life would be."

MY MOTHER TAUGHT ME MANY things, but if there was one thing I learned from my father, it was the meaning of *respect.* I recall one particular Sunday morning when I just didn't want to get out of bed to get ready for church. I had been allowed to stay up late the night before to watch an old movie, and I was hoping my father might let me sleep in just a little while longer. Of course, I knew that was wishful thinking, as improbable as Mother permitting me to be late for school. I was an altar boy, and punctual attendance was not only necessary, it was mandatory.

Turning over to enjoy my last moments of uninterrupted slumber, I heard the familiar sound of my bedroom door opening, and I knew my father's voice would not be far behind. "Kimasho!" *Let's go*! He always called to me in Japanese. "Rise and shine!"

It was a morning game we played, and I'd respond with a Japanese phrase I had begged him to teach me, "Mo sugu desu!" *Soon!*

"Ima!" *Now!*

I'd start laughing and counter with another phrase, "Ato de, *Later . . .* Dozo!" *please!.* This game would continue until I respected his wishes (or ran out of Japanese phrases).

My father, Theodore Popovich, was the son of Eastern European immigrants and truly a man for all seasons. Father, friend, counselor, soldier, linguist and chess player extraordinaire, he was a man of impeccable humanitarian credentials and inherent humility.

My father was the silent force, which shaped my basic understanding of the value he most guarded and cherished: Respect for one's self and that of others.

Over breakfast, Father announced the day's agenda: Church, dinner, and a visit to the New Brighton home of his Aunt Sara. Anticipating my usual protest, he said, "You know, Robert, it's very important to pay your respects to your relatives."

I nodded agreeably and continued eating as though I didn't care that visiting Father's Aunt Sara would consist of spending a hot summer afternoon perched on an itchy horsehair sofa in an old Victorian house on my best behavior. He looked at me, puzzled.

However, I had thought about the fact that Aunt Sara was pleasant, kind and so appreciative for the time we spent with her. In addition, she always had candy and soft drinks, which were not on my parents' list of household essentials. So, I wasn't at all averse to going.

On our way home from that visit, Father was pleased. He said he was happy that we found Aunt Sara to be in good spirits and perfect health, and then he looked at me with curiosity.

"Robert, I think you also enjoyed the afternoon," he said, obviously surprised by my lack of a morose attitude.

"It wasn't too bad," I replied.

"So, what made this visit different from all the other times we went there?" he prodded.

"Maybe I'm learning that it's important to spend time with family," I told him. I was beginning to internalize and understand his feelings about respect.

Father often said, "Respect takes a lifetime to build, but only a second to lose. No matter how unfair that may seem, it's logical that we should take great care to protect others' respect for us at all times."

I was in college when he uttered those exact words, and I asked him, "How can anyone feel comfortable with that constant threat in mind?"

"It isn't as terrible as it might seem," he said before offering these words of advice: "Think—*before* you speak or act. Take into account the potential consequences of your actions, and you'll rarely have a problem." I found his explanation realistic and satisfying.

After entering the corporate world and subsequently becoming a consultant, I struggled with Father's concept of respect and the role I perceived it played in business. In the business world, it appeared as though an individual's title, function and performance record seemed to define the respect others felt for him or her. In fact, such shallow assessments usually spilled into social settings, as well. Cocktail conversations often began with leading questions, like '*What school did you attend?*' and '*Where do you live?*' that were designed to elicit answers about how much money you make and how well connected you might be.

I was dismayed to conclude that the respect a person commanded appeared reduced to the size of his or her portfolio. This realization shook my faith and challenged Father's teachings until an unfortunate incident occurred that would renew my faith.

I was attending a retreat for a professional firm, when one of their esteemed senior partners put on a display of impropriety that rivaled any I had ever witnessed. Clearly drunk, this man began making prejudiced comments that touched every level of society. As if that weren't enough, he also told jokes that could only be defined as base and a total misunderstanding of the intent of humor.

Throughout the evening, his behavior became so obnoxious that people at other tables were becoming visibly annoyed. It wasn't long before he finally excused himself and left the room.

Sitting at our table was another partner, two associates, two administrative assistants and two important clients. I made no comment, but it was clear that the group at our table felt a sense of relief and acute embarrassment. One of the administrative assistants even offered apologies on behalf of the firm, and the second assistant echoed her remarks.

"His behavior is not representative of his true nature," She assured, and one of the clients smiled politely; subsequent discussion centered on general topics until the other client unexpectedly brought up the subject of propriety in society. "How important is it, these days, to show consideration and respect for others?" he mused, and everyone at the table began to chime in. For the next hour, the discussion ranged from the need to reevaluate the values that are truly important in life and business to the responsibility that each of us has—no matter what level or position we attain—to maintain self-respect and respect for others.

I believe that this conversation probably would not have taken place without the performance of the inebriated senior partner. His behavior served as a vivid demonstration of the results of discarding respect.

I never heard whether he suffered any negative feedback within the firm, but based upon Father's teachings, I can't imagine any punishment worse than that of lowering his own self-esteem. What I can assume, however, is that the people seated at our table and the others who witnessed his behavior may forgive, but they won't soon forget. It is virtually assured that the lofty level of respect he had prior to the luncheon has plummeted.

As father said, "Respect takes a lifetime to build and only a second to lose." However, I learned something else from that experience: I was pleased to know that the basic ingredients of Father's definition of respect are *not* in danger of giving way to the changing times.

EXTRA EFFORT

Mother always said, "Robert . . .
*if you give more than is asked of you,
you most often receive more in return.'*

MY PARENTS' WORK ETHIC WAS a result of their heritage. It went beyond the standard cliché' of *a fair day's pay for a fair day's work.* Mother was taught that if you give *more* than what is expected, you would never want—nor will your employer—for reward or recognition.

"What do you mean by 'give *more*'?" I once asked her.

"*More* means keeping a positive attitude and taking initiative," she explained, but I still didn't get it. So she said, "Look, Robert, just remember that whenever you are given a task, always try to do *more* than what is expected, and never ask for or expect instant rewards for your efforts. Just know that rewards can come quickly, but at other times, they may take much longer. However, they will eventually come." Not soon after this talk, I had a concrete example land in my lap in the form of garbage.

When I was a youngster, one of my daily tasks was taking out the garbage. So, each day I did just that—no more, no less. One day, I noticed a strong odor emanating from the waste can. Holding my nose, it became clear that something *more* had to be done: the garbage can needed to be washed out as well as emptied.

In addition to emptying the garbage and washing out the can, I also sprayed the can with disinfectant. Mother observed my effort and pulled out the mixer and pans. When I was finished, she said, "I just want to thank you for doing more than what was asked. I'm making your favorite apple pie, and it should be done in an hour."

Although I appreciated the praise and reward, I felt an equally strong feeling of self-satisfaction and accomplishment. Extra effort means going that extra mile, but little did I know that one day it would require me to go an additional 4,000 miles, just to prove that I had not forgotten the lesson.

I had just arrived in New York after an exhausting six-week trip through four Eastern-Block countries. I was physically and emotionally drained. The passport and visa requirements alone can tax the most seasoned traveler, and this particular trip was even worse.

My only thought was to return home for a much-needed rest. However, as I waited for my luggage to arrive in the baggage claim area, I heard an announcement on the intercom: "Your attention, please. Passenger Mr. Robert Popovich, please contact the Pan Am message desk immediately." I heard my name, but the page did not register for a moment. Then it was repeated, I eventually realized I was the one being paged. My first thought came in the form of a question, *how could anyone know on which flight I would be arriving?* I couldn't imagine who it might be.

It turned out to be my secretary. Over the phone, she told me that one of my clients had called in a barely-controlled state of panic and needed to speak with me immediately. She didn't know the specifics, but she had a number for me to call. After several busy signals, I finally reached him.

"Robert!" He exclaimed as soon as he heard my voice. "Boy am I glad to hear from you! I need to ask you to do me a big favor."

As long as it doesn't have to happen for at least forty-eight hours! I thought, but sure enough, he wanted me to fly to Pittsburgh that evening and then immediately on to Phoenix, Arizona. I couldn't believe what I was hearing. What could be so important?

With great urgency in his voice, he explained, "My company is entertaining a senior delegation of German officials at our Phoenix office *tomorrow*. I was hoping you could provide us with translation and protocol support. I understand if this is too short notice for you, but I wouldn't be asking if it weren't critical."

"I'll do it," I told him, despite my desire to go home, crawl in bed and sleep for days.

He met me at the terminal as soon as I arrived in Pittsburgh's airport. I was briefed on the situation as we walked to the next flight.

"Our flight to Phoenix will be enjoyable," he assured me. He had booked us on a nonstop, first-class flight, so that we would be able to relax and discuss the details over dinner.

This was not at all, what happened.

As we checked in at the ticket counter, we were advised that our flight to Phoenix was canceled, and we could only be rebooked on another flight that was leaving two hours later. Further, the only available seats were in coach, and no meal would be served. Then we learned that the flight would be going to Tucson, and we would have to drive to Phoenix.

By the time we arrived in Tucson, it was midnight. Another surrealistic four hours of driving a rental car through the darkened desert and we finally pulled into our hotel at four o'clock in the morning, which gave us only one hour to rest before we had to get ready to head for the office.

At the office that morning, I somehow managed to prepare a brief agenda and protocol requirements on little to no sleep. At 7 a.m., I advised senior management that we should be outside when the German delegation arrived. Manners dictated this move, but once we stepped outside, I found the cool morning air to be a much-needed elixir.

The agenda I put together was straightforward: We began with an initial tour of the facility, followed by preliminary discussions, then a break for lunch and after which more meetings were held.

As the sessions proceeded, it became apparent that some members of the delegation had a stronger command of the English language than others. My role was to provide intermediary support as needed, and the sessions went quite well, with both parties more than satisfied with the outcome. At the end of the day, we exchanged farewells and business cards. It was now time to return to New York City for a much-needed rest.

My client insisted on taking me to the airport, and as we were about to leave the office, he turned to me and expressed his personal thanks and appreciation. Then he added, "You know Robert, everything happened so fast, we never got around to discussing your fee."

"Well, it wasn't of major importance at the time," I replied.

He smiled and handed me a sealed envelope. "I hope you find the compensation acceptable," he said, adding, "Please open it and tell me if this is okay with you."

I just put the envelope into my jacket pocket and returned his smile. "I'm sure you were more than fair," I told him.

When he dropped me off at the airport, he again expressed his gratitude. "I know this wasn't easy for you, and I really appreciate the fact that you went above and beyond the call of ordinary business expectations."

"It was demanding," I acknowledged, thinking that the rings around my eyes probably spoke for themselves. "The most important thing is that it all turned out well for everyone." We both knew that his bringing me in on the talks with the Germans would guarantee my role as an integral part of future agreements, which would establish a bond between our two countries. I also appreciated the fact that I would now have more contacts in Germany. In addition, I considered his strong desire to have me involved in these talks as the highest form of professional respect. I believed that I had already been compensated in abundance, regardless of the monetary amount.

I was back on the airplane and waiting for the plane to take off when it suddenly occurred to me to check out what was in that envelope. I reached inside my left front suit pocket and pulled it out, not expecting the munificent sum within. I looked at the amount and realized that just as I had given more than what was expected, they had written a check that was more than generous. And so it goes.

VALUE

Mother always said, "Robert . . .
value is something everyone looks for in everything, they buy or experience in their lives."

I WAS FACING ONE OF THE most difficult decisions in my young life and I had to choose between buying a new Boy Scout uniform versus replacing my old, worn-out bike. My mind was spinning like a little voice on my left shoulder kept whispering, "Take the bike! It's so much fun! Besides, you know you'll need it for your paper route."

On the other shoulder was the collective voice of my entire scout troop reminding me, "It's almost jamboree time, and every scout in the entire United States will be there! You'll look great with all of your merit badges sewn on your bright, new uniform."

At dinnertime I sat motionless before my plate; uninterested in eating, which Mother knew was a clear sign that I was facing a dilemma of overwhelming proportions.

"Is something wrong?" she questioned.

I said nothing.

"You're looking awfully sad," she observed.

Aside from an almost undetectable shrug of my shoulders, I remained inaccessible.

"If you're so troubled, can't you tell me why?" she asked before sitting down in front of me to wait it out.

After a while, I finally muttered, "It wouldn't do any good anyway."

Mother leaned forward, knowing that whenever I made that statement, I was right on the brink of sharing. As expected, I began to spill my guts about the uniform-versus-the-bike debate.

After listening to my tale of woe,

"I can certainly understand why you're so troubled, Robert. That's a tough choice!" she commiserated before launching into, "How do you think you're going to solve this problem?"

"I don't know," I whined, miserably. "I was hoping you could make up my mind for me."

"I could, but I won't," she said, predictably. "Robert, the freedom of personal choice is very precious; it shouldn't be easily relinquished, even in the most difficult of times."

I thought that was a cop-out, but I wasn't going to tell her that.

She then said, "Let me ask you this—which do you think is more important: the bicycle or the uniform?"

I couldn't say. Seeing my frustration, Mother suggested I list the benefits of each.

I did so, and it was helpful, but this did not result in a solution. Since it was getting late, Mother recommended I go to bed and sleep on it.

The next morning, I walked into the kitchen where Mother was preparing breakfast and announced that I'd come to a decision.

"I chose the uniform," I told her, adding, "and making that decision was much easier than I had originally thought. My paper route can survive with my old bike, but scouting is something special, so it has greater value."

I realized that some of my most memorable moments had occurred in scouting; the things I had learned and the friends I had made were priceless. Scouting was an adventure, while a bike was just transportation, and my commitment to the uniform symbolized my basic priorities and interests.

I thanked Mother for helping and asked her what her choice would have been.

"I would also choose the uniform," she answered.

"Why? I asked her.

"For all the same reasons you did," she replied. Then she explained, "In business, the product's value is in the eye of the beholder . . . in other words, the customer, and if the customer isn't in agreement with your perception of what a product is worth, then you need to find out why. After acknowledging the customer's point of view, you must set about trying to broaden their understanding of why the price is what it is. This is not always an easy task, but if skillfully handled, it can bring positive results."

Years later, I experienced an incident I fondly recall as, *Oil and Water Can Sometimes Mix*

While working on an assignment in Paris, in between work, I often liked to stroll up and down the Seine River, observing the artists and artisans practicing their vocations. On one occasion, I witnessed a memorable performance when a watercolor artist recreated a realistic rendition of Notre Dame Cathedral with skilled dexterity at an astonishing speed.

As I watched this amazing feat of artistry, I noticed that another person was as enthralled as me. He was tall, lean and handsome, approximately 50 years of age, and his clothing came right out of an old American cowboy movie. I guessed that he must have been successful in either oil or ranching.

Since he was standing right next to me, I asked him, "What do you think of his painting?"

No response. I thought that perhaps he was too absorbed in what he was observing to reply to me, but I could hear him muttering. As his words grew in volume and intensity, I was able to detect what sounded like, "Ain't he the best dawg-gone somethin' you ever did see!"

Although it was asked rhetorically, I saw it as an opportunity to try again to strike up a conversation. "He certainly is!" I agreed.

Apparently surprised by the unanticipated response, he turned and looked curiously at me as though he just noticed I was there. "Oh, do you like him, too?" The ice had been broken.

I soon learned that his name was Terry Long, and sure enough, he was an oilman from Texas on vacation in Paris. He said that he intended to purchase an original French painting. I couldn't help but smile at this confirmation of my assumptions. I was impressed by his humility and sincere appreciation for what he was observing.

As we talked, the artist continued to work; his deformed, apparently arthritic fingers moved with painful purpose across the canvas. His wrinkle-rimmed eyes focused with an intensity that obviously blocked out everything except the task at hand, which included the two of us watching. In a matter of only two hours, he had completed a beautiful and remarkably detailed replica of Notre Dame.

As the old man put the finishing touches on his painting, my newfound acquaintance could no longer restrain his enthusiasm. "That paintin' is absolutely incredible!" he exclaimed. "I gotta' have it!"

He approached the artist and pulled out his wallet as he asked, "How much do you want for it, sir?"

The Frenchman slowly turned and said in a soft, polite, but matter-of-fact voice, "Five-hundred American dollars" before returning his attention to his work.

The Texan's smile quickly melted. "Five hundred dollars for two 'ours a' work?" he cried. "That's two-hundred an' fifty dollars an hour!"

His brush hovered above the canvas as the artist quietly addressed the customer's outrage. "You are correct, monsieur," he said. "From that point of view, it is a lot of money."

The Texan looked pleased but confused by the artist's response.

The painter continued, "Monsieur would you like to know why I charge so much?"

"Uhhh! Well . . . yes."

Then, in a patient and polite tone of voice, the old man recounted the many years he'd spent studying art all over France and Europe, including the endless hours of practicing and painting the same scenes over and over again.

"So you see, monsieur, I've devoted 50 years of my life to be able to paint such a scene in only two hours, and from that point of view, I think $500 is a bargain. What do you think?"

"I'll take it," said the Texan.

I envisioned Mr. Long taking the painting home and hanging it in a conspicuous space for all to see. I imagined that the painting's originality and beauty would prompt the obvious questions: *Who painted it? How did you come to purchase it? How long did it take an artist to complete?* And then the ultimate question: *How much did it cost?* That would elicit the obvious comment, expressed in an incredulous tone: *That's a lot of money for just two hours of work!*

I imagined that the Texan would then turn to his guest and say in a patient and polite tone of voice, "Do ya' wanna know *why* I paid $500 for just two hours of work?"

Value is ultimately based upon each individual's perceptions and expectations. The ability to influence others is largely determined by how well we accurately identify these factors. In addition, a natural evolution takes place in each of us, as we grow older. What had little value in our youth may become very important later in our lives.

I've learned that some values are more priceless than any work of art: They are the personal beliefs and principles by which we judge ourselves and are ultimately judged by others.

LOYALTY

Mother always said, "Robert . . .
loyalty is standing beside someone doing the best of times, and more importantly, during the worst of times."

WHEN MOTHER'S EMPLOYER, MORRIS CHAMOVITZ, spoke of her, he would always mention her commitment and loyalty. "I've never had a more loyal employee!" he would say.

In my early teens, I assumed loyalty meant that someone is hardworking and trusted. In addition, when Mr. Chamovitz again commented on how loyal my mother was, I asked him, "What does loyalty mean to you?"

"I don't have an easy or quick answer for you, Robert," he admitted. Then he looked at me with interest, and asked, "What do *you* think it means?"

Based on my limited experience, I replied, "I think that loyalty results when two people respect and support one another."

"That's a big part of it," he agreed, "but there's much more to it." Just as he was about to tell me what that "much more" was, we were interrupted, and the discussion was never finished.

Years later, I was having lunch with Mother, and I was telling her about one of my clients. "He says he's having trouble teaching his employees loyalty," I told her, explaining that he had hired a behavioral-science consulting firm to assess the relative level of loyalty and make recommendations for improving it.

Mother shook her head, "Well, the first thing he did wrong was to hire a firm, and the second was to assume that loyalty can be programmed into people."

At that moment, it reminded of the question I had asked Morris so many years ago. I recalled the conversation and asked mother if she would care to try and to express his feelings. After all, he had been her mentor, and they shared similar beliefs.

"Although I felt a deep sense of obligation and appreciation for his having hired me, I also knew that his action wasn't out of sympathy," Mother explained. "It was based upon a sound business decision, and we both gained something in the exchange.

"My loyalty to him developed out of the daily events; both personal and business-related, that I was confronted with. Loyalty isn't created through a written policy or direct order, and you don't instigate situations to test or promote it, either. It's something that is developed over time, and it must be *earned*," she emphasized.

"Loyalty begins with the business and personal philosophy of management *and* the employees," she said, noting, "The closer those beliefs are, the greater the chance of developing a foundation for loyalty."

Mother added that for her, the most important issues were having an opportunity to work, to be judged fairly and rewarded for her efforts, while gaining an education from someone she liked and respected.

"Loyalty also has a lot to do with the human sensitivity demonstrated by management toward workers," Mother added. "For example, when your father was ill, Morris was always offering assistance. I was too proud to accept his charity, but I never forgot his sincere thoughtfulness. He also had a sixth sense when something was wrong, and when it was appropriate to offer advice or help, he would. But that's just one side of the story."

Then she spoke of another aspect of loyalty. "It wasn't about money or bonuses; it was the respect he showed me in every situation," she explained. "Regardless of whether it was in front of an irate customer or in management meetings with his partner and staff, he always treated me as an equal. In fact, he would often say, 'Dolly (Morris' nickname for Mother), titles just tell you what people do. They don't tell you how much of a contribution they are making or how devoted they are.'"

Then she brought up education. Mother had never graduated from high school, so Mr. Chamovitz took it upon himself to tutor her and help her become an astute and professional businesswoman. He once told her, "Dolly, you always had the right ingredients to succeed; I just happened to be the one to offer a recipe. Never forget that it was you, and you alone, who baked the cake."

"I appreciated what he said, but I pointed out to him no one can do it alone; and even if they could, they shouldn't," said Mother. "It's the sharing that makes it so special."

When it came to her career, Mother was promoted based upon her performance, and not her years of service. Her ability as a businesswoman, manager and confidant was something of an anomaly in her day, as was her boss's progressive attitude. Gender was never an issue with Morris. He would often say, "The only true way of measuring the differences in people is how well they perform. Other than that, I only see another human being."

When it came to Mother, he would say, "Whatever goals I set for the stores she managed; I could always count on her to do her best to achieve them, which she usually did. She was the best employee I ever had, and her fellow workers adored her."

I finally understood why Morris couldn't offer a simple definition. The development of loyalty depends upon the way that companies define their basic philosophy, as well as, how they word their mission statements and integrate them into their organizations.

If a company's philosophy is practiced on a daily basis, the mission statement will become a living document—not a symbolic representation of intent. Loyalty by decree will never be meaningful.

Several days after that conversation with Mother, I visited my forlorn loyalty client, now feeling much better equipped to advise him. I asked him a series of questions about the longevity of his employees; their attitude when they entered the company and when they left; the relationship between upper and front-line management and lower-level employees; the types and nature of discussions held during the normal course of the workday; how much management knew about the employees beyond their resumes and work performance; and, finally, what kinds of company events might be established to promote relationship-building that would be positively received and well-attended. His answers were vague and unsure "What would you suggest we do?" he asked me, clearly ready to hire me on the spot.

"I don't think I would be the answer," I told him.

He gave me a puzzled look. "Then what is the answer?"

Without missing a beat, I told him, "I'd like to figuratively introduce you to two people I've grown to know quite well in my life: The first is my mother, and the second was her employer."

He looked at me in disbelief, but he didn't say a word as I continued to tell him about loyalty, as it was taught to me.

Several weeks later, I received a phone call from him. "I want to take your mother to lunch," he told me.

"Why?" I asked him, and he told me that her second-hand advice worked.

"So, I want to take her out to lunch," he repeated.

"Hey, wait a minute," I quipped, "*I* was the one who told you the story!"

"You're right," he replied, grinning. "But your mother was the one who *wrote* it. Should I reward the author or the messenger?"

"Well, you know the messenger is usually shot," I retorted.

"So, consider yourself lucky!" he replied, good-naturedly.

In fact, writing this book has made me my mother's messenger. It has been a pleasure to share these experiences with you, and to acknowledge, not only my mother for her unselfishness and dedication to her family, friends and community, but also to all of the countless mothers in the world who have done the same.

Epilogue

First—no one holds the set of keys to opening the doors of life's infinite mysteries and endless challenges—all the more reason to cherish the knowledge and experiences of past generations.

Second—that everyone and everything on this Earth has a purpose, value, and natural order—it is when we disrupt this chain of life that problems begin.

Third—*vision* is the ability to see beyond the obvious—how can we gain a different perspective to solve our problems? ***"Stand on the Moon and look back at the Earth,"*** and a new perspective will quickly come into view.

Fourth—respect all things and all people—not just out of an externally imposed code of conduct and legal obligations, but from an internally directed desire to be a person of honor, substance, word and deed.

Fifth—look for the *good* in others—don't becoming a victim of cynicism, jealousy, selfishness and anger. For in the end, we are all measured by the good we have done.

Sixth—don't take ourselves too seriously—for in the final analysis, we are but a 'nano-second' in universal time.

Seventh—set goals higher than what is expected of us, and we are all but assured of reaching those former goals. Our degree of effort is directly proportionate to the goals we set.

Eighth—most people hope for success, while those who achieve it never hope for it, they *just do it.* Set the goal, set it high—stay disciplined and focused—and you will never be denied.

Ninth—don't forget the true meaning and priceless value of family, friends and relationships—for happiness and success were never meant to be experienced alone; the happiness to be shared.

Tenth—wisdom and hope reside within each of us, but we occasionally need to reflect upon and give thanks to those special individuals who have contributed to placing them there.

BY POPULAR DEMAND . . . Coming Soon! We have received countless requests from around the world, asking for more of Mother's wisdom. **Volume I** covers the author's experiences from 1965 to 1990. I'm pleased to announce, that **Volumes II & III** will cover the author's adventures between the years 1991 to 2014. The stories include, harrowing experiences in Russia and Siberia, West & East Berlin, West Germany, Ireland, France, Italy and South America. It's a roller coaster ride with mother at the helm—if you enjoyed Volume I, Volumes II & III are just around the corner.

Printed in the United States
by Baker & Taylor Publisher Services